SCRIPTURE PATHWAYS TO INNER HEALING

VICTOR M. PARACHIN

LIGUORI
PUBLICATIONS

One Liguori Drive
Liguori, MO 63057-9999
(314) 464-2500

ISBN 0-89243-591-7
Library of Congress Catalog Card Number: 94-75227

Copyright © 1994, Victor M. Parachin
Printed in the United States of America

Except where otherwise noted, Scripture quotations are taken from
the *Good News Bible,* copyright © American Bible Society 1966,
1971, 1976. Used with permission. All rights reserved.

Cover design by Wendy Barnes

CONTENTS

Ten Healing Movements

SUNDAY
Deciding to Make Changes

"The Kingdom of God is within you."
Luke 17:21

In this seven-word statement, Jesus reminds us that God is working in each life; that the kingdom of God produces new people. Jesus assures us that God's power works within us to transcend external circumstances. Therefore, there is ample reason to hope for a better future.

However, for God's work to be effective in our lives, we need to cooperate. And the most effective way of cooperating with God is simply making a decision to change. Although our inner child has been bruised and battered, we can begin the healing process by deciding to make changes. Here is an A-B-C-D method for change.

A. *Acknowledge the hurt.* People who should have loved you, nurtured you, and protected you have, in fact, hurt you. Acknowledge what was done to you. Be aware of the pain, the loss, and the grief.

B. *Believe you can overcome.* Move directly from a timid, hesitant outlook to one of vibrant hope. Believe that you have the resources to overcome all past pains. Believe that God can help you day by day.

C. *Commit to recovery.* Tell yourself over and over and over again that you can change the impact of what happened.

Remind yourself that your past is not going to be your future. Keep saying to yourself, *I'll do whatever it takes.*

D. *Develop an action plan.* Get any help that you need to recover. Confide in a trusted friend, seek out a gifted counselor, join a support group, develop your spiritual life. Make a plan and follow it.

PRAYER

Loving God, I thank you that your kingdom of hope, love, and peace can rise from within my life. Day by day, guide me and let me experience your kingdom. Amen.

AFFIRMATIONS

Today I will stand up to despair.

Today I will be less hesitant and more hopeful.

Today I will have faith in myself and in my God.

REFLECTION

"Every noble work is at first impossible."

Thomas Carlyle

MONDAY

Harnessing the Power of Hope

"…hold firmly to the hope placed before us."
Hebrews 6:18

In 1966 a group of fanatical Chinese teenagers called the Red Guard broke into the house of Nien Cheng. After looting her home, they arrested her as an "enemy of the people." Nien Cheng would spend the next seven years imprisoned and in solitary confinement. In her book *Life and Death in Shanghai*, she shares this glorious experience.

> Throughout the years of my imprisonment, I had turned to God and often felt His presence. In the drab surroundings of the gray cell, I had known magic moments of transcendence that I had not experienced in the ease and comfort of my normal life. My faith had sustained me in these the darkest hours of my life and brought me safely through privation, sickness, and torture.

The experience Nien Cheng describes is what the Bible calls *hope*. The word is used hundreds of times in the Scriptures and is found in almost every book of the Bible. It can be defined as confidence in God's rescuing power and redeeming love. Hold on to the biblical truth that God's hope can penetrate and transform the most damaged life and the most desperate situation.

PRAYER

Merciful and kind God, fill me with hope. Help me trust you day by day. Restore my confidence in your redeeming love and rescuing power, even in my life. Amen.

AFFIRMATIONS

I will press ahead filled with hope.

I will do whatever it takes.

I will resolve the issues.

REFLECTION

Live in faith and hope, though it be in darkness. Cast your care on God for you are His and He will not forget you. Do not think that He is leaving you alone, for that would be wrong to Him.

Saint John of the Cross

TUESDAY
Cultivating Daily Hope

This is the day that the LORD has made;
let us rejoice and be glad in it.
Psalm 118:24
(*New Revised Standard Version*)

This short verse from Psalm 118 tells us how to cultivate hope. It tells us to hope for the moment. Behind these words is the knowledge that there are times when it is hard to believe that we have a bright future. The writers of Scripture knew that we all experience moments when we are simply not brave enough or strong enough. When these times come, we are instructed to concentrate on the present: *This is the day that the Lord has made.*

Until our courage and optimism return, we are to focus only on the events of this hour and this day. If we cannot anticipate a bright, happy future, we can look to the beauty present right now:

- the vibrant, warm sunshine

- a well-prepared meal

- the ability to see, hear, and speak

- the pleasure of a good book

- the blooming of flowers

- the beauty of the dawn and the dusk

- the joy of children at play
- the presence of a good friend
- the kindness of a neighbor

The words of Psalm 118 remind us to sink our roots deeply into the present until the possibility of thinking about an optimistic tomorrow develops.

PRAYER

Loving God, help me to see the beauty of the present moment. Open the eyes of my soul to see the many good things you send me moment by moment, hour by hour, and day by day. Amen.

AFFIRMATIONS

Today I will see the beauty all around.

Today I will sense God's loving presence.

Today I will rejoice in my life.

REFLECTION

Happiness depends upon ourselves.

Aristotle

WEDNESDAY
Saying Yes When Life Shouts No

Be strong, be courageous, all you that hope in the LORD.
Psalm 31:24

Interestingly, modern researchers confirm the insight of Scripture, which has always recognized that hope is a dynamic energy for living. According to Daniel Goleman, Ph.D., a psychologist and author,

> Hope helps a lot more than many of us ever thought it could. Rigorous new studies identify hope as a powerful positive, force in human endeavor—a secret ingredient that can help nurture your health, well-being and success.

Because of its power to anchor and renew life, hope is cited as one of the three pillars of Christianity, along with faith and love. Hope helps us say yes when life shouts no. In the Bible, hope and survival are inseparably linked, as in the following passages:

Be strong, be courageous,
all you that hope in the LORD.

Psalm 31:24

It was by hope that we were saved.

Romans 8:24

Consider the experience of twenty-five thousand American soldiers held captive by the Japanese during World War II.

Forced to exist under extreme conditions, many died. Yet others survived to return home after the war. The survivors were different in only one major aspect: they lived with the hope of release someday. In the book *Holding on to Hope*, Robin Reader observes:

> They [the survivors] talked about the kind of homes they would have, the jobs they would choose, and even described the kind of persons they would marry. They drew pictures on the walls to illustrate their dreams. The doctors taken captive even formed medical societies.

There is an important lesson in the experience of these prisoners of war. The hope of a better tomorrow can help us deal with the difficulties today.

PRAYER

Merciful God, help me choose to respond hopefully even though life has treated me harshly. Remind me of Jesus, who ministered with faith, hope, and love in spite of his suffering. Amen.

AFFIRMATIONS

God has created an abundant, satisfying universe.

I accept God's abundance for me today.

God's blessings and riches flow freely into my life today.

REFLECTION

I find that the great thing in this world is not so much where we stand as in what direction we are moving.

Oliver Wendell Holmes

THURSDAY
Using Hope to Cope

*"I alone know the plans
I have for you,
plans to bring you prosperity
and not disaster,
plans to bring about the future you hope for."*
Jeremiah 29:11

Timothy Elliott, Ph.D., a psychologist at Virginia Commonwealth University, studies the dynamics of hope. For one of his hope projects, Dr. Elliott interviewed fifty-seven young victims of spinal-cord injuries, all of whom were paralyzed for life. He discovered that the most hopeful patients were the least depressed and had managed to gain greater physical mobility. Those who held on to hope were also more socially active. Clearly, hoping leads to better coping.

This is especially true for Christians because hope is grounded in the confident expectation that God is working for our good. No matter how tangled our lives become, no matter how painful our issues, no matter how devastating the blows of life, God is present to anchor, stabilize, and guide us safely through.

PRAYER

Loving God, let hope rise and flow freely from my life. Let me awaken each day more hopeful, more joyful, more peaceful. Amen.

AFFIRMATIONS

This is the day the Lord has made.

I will rejoice in it.

I trust God to renew my life.

REFLECTION

Sometimes we are unduly excited when things go well, and at other times we are too alarmed when things go badly....We ought to establish our hearts firmly in God's strength and struggle, as best we can, to place all of our hope and confidence in the Lord.

Jordan of Saxony

FRIDAY
Hope Differs From Optimism

We put our hope in the LORD;
he is our protector and our help.
Psalm 33:20

An optimist takes a cheerful view of all events. Although a person with hope may also have that view of life, hope differs from optimism because it is grounded in the reality of God. Behind hope is the understanding that God works to bring good out of evil, blessing out of burden, and even triumph out of tragedy. That is why writers of Scripture, such as the Psalmist quoted at the beginning of today's meditation, are consistent in linking hope with belief in God. Here is what biblical hope can do for you:

- Hope expects good to emerge from events rather than concentrating on the worst that has happened.

- Hope opens doors where despair slams them shut.

- Hope sees a cup as half full rather than half empty.

- Hope sets priorities and goals and moves toward them relentlessly.

- Hope lights a candle rather than cursing the darkness.

- Hope views life as a creative challenge, not a meaningless series of problems.

- Hope is patient and understands that true growth takes time.

- Hope takes loss in stride, knowing that God assures ultimate victory.

- Hope moves forward, refusing to quit and give up.

PRAYER

Loving God, thank you for not abandoning me. Day by day, help me continue to believe you are working on my behalf. Day by day, set before me the example of Jesus, in whom is the most powerful demonstration of good over evil. Amen.

AFFIRMATIONS

I affirm that with God nothing is impossible.
I affirm that God's love is supporting me, sustaining me, and strengthening me.
I affirm that life holds great promise.

REFLECTION

If it were not for hopes, the heart would break.

Thomas Fuller

SATURDAY
Managing Our Feelings

But I had nearly lost confidence;
my faith was almost gone.
Psalm 73:2

Feeling the stresses and strains of life, a young Midwestern lawyer entered the following words in his journal:

> I am now the most miserable man living. If what I feel were equally distributed to the whole human family, there would not be one cheerful face on earth. Whether I shall ever be better I cannot tell. To remain as I am is impossible; I must die or be better, it appears to me.

Those words were written in 1841 by Abraham Lincoln. Because of his depressed emotional state, Lincoln's family and friends thought it wise to keep knives, razors, and other sharp objects out of his reach. In addition, they had someone stay with him through the nights, fearing that he would take his life if left alone.

Of course, Lincoln survived that dark time in his life and went on to become one of the country's greatest presidents. For those who struggle with depression and despair, there are three important and inspiring lessons to be learned from Lincoln's experience.

1. Feelings are never permanent.

2. Time is a great healer.

3. The best course is to be patient and wait for relief. Managing our feelings, rather than having our feelings manage us, is critical to making the transition from hesitation to hope.

PRAYER

Loving God, when I am feeling depressed and discouraged, help me to be patient. Give me the faith to believe that feelings of depression will pass and that the clouds over my life will give way to sunshine. Amen.

AFFIRMATIONS

The steadfast love of God fills me;
I am filled with peace.
The wisdom of God illuminates my life; I think clearly.
The strength of God flows to me; I am confident.

REFLECTION

No emotion, any more than a wave, can long retain its own individual form.

Henry Ward Beecher

SUNDAY

Minimizing Fear by Maximizing Prayer

"Do not be afraid."
Matthew 10:31

Fear is a powerful adversary. Whenever it manifests in our lives, it emerges as a bully—intimidating and powerful. It is no wonder that Jesus often told people not to be afraid. In fact, one of the most common phrases in the Bible is "fear not."

While strength and courage come to people in various ways, meditation and prayer can calm the soul, instill courage, and reduce fear. Someone has rightly noted that we are prey to our fears until we pray fear away.

It was through prayer that Colonel Robinson Risner was able to minimize his fears and endure seven years as a POW in North Vietnam. An Air Force pilot, Risner was shot down in September 1965. He would not see his wife and his five children until February 20, 1973. In his book *The Passing of the Night*, Risner tells how prayer helped him deal with fear, torture, and isolation: "I prayed God would give me strength to endure it. When it would get so bad that I couldn't take it, I would ask God to ease it and somehow I would make it. He kept me."

The same power that minimized fear and strengthened Risner is available to us through prayer.

PRAYER

Kind and gracious God, fill me with your spirit of power, strength, and courage. Help me to live more with faith and less with fear. Amen.

AFFIRMATIONS

I feel the presence of God's power.

I have a special relationship with God.

I reclaim my natural ability to trust God.

REFLECTION

Aspire to God with short but frequent outpourings of the heart; admire his bounty; invoke his aid; cast yourself in spirit at the foot of his cross; adore his goodness; give him your whole soul a thousand times a day.

Saint Francis de Sales

MONDAY
God Illuminates Our Darkness

*"Our God is merciful and tender.
He will cause the bright dawn
of salvation to rise on us...."*
Luke 1:78

People whose inner child has been hurt often describe their lives in terms of great darkness. While that description is accurate, it should be balanced by the fact that God is merciful and tender and is present in all of life to illuminate the darkness. The truth is, people can move through the darkness.

Consider the following courageous women and men who moved through their dark times:

- *Ludwig van Beethoven.* In spite of the darkness of deafness, he continued to produce some of the greatest music the world has ever known.

- *Abraham Lincoln.* He lead the splintered nation through the darkness of slavery and the Civil War.

- *Helen Keller.* Blinded and deafened as a child, she moved through the darkness and learned to communicate, attended a university, wrote books, lectured worldwide, and became a source of inspiration to thousands.

- *Winston Churchill.* He struggled personally with a severe lifelong depression yet inspired and moved an

entire nation through the darkest hours of World
War II.

- *Franklin Delano Roosevelt.* Crippled and partially
  paralyzed by polio, he guided the nation through the
  dark years of the Great Depression.

- *Viktor Frankl.* He lived through the shadows of gas
  chambers and the darkness of concentration camps
  and went on to become a psychiatrist whose innovative views have helped liberate thousands of minds.

- *Martin Luther King.* A victim of bias himself, he
  marched with millions to reduce the darkness of
  racism and prejudice.

Like these and so many others, you, too, can move through
the dark feelings of bereavement and grief.

PRAYER

*Loving and gracious God, calm the waves of my heart, silence the storms of my spirit, dispel the darkness of my life.
Amen.*

AFFIRMATIONS

Today I am peaceful.

Today I wait patiently for God to dispel darkness.

Today I do not fear the darkness.

REFLECTION

*For each and for all…the watchword should be "Carry on,
and dread nought."*

Winston Churchill

TUESDAY
God Transforms Lead Into Gold

*"Even though you intended to do harm to me,
God intended it for good...."*
Genesis 50:20
(New Revised Standard Version)

Consider this ancient story from China. A peasant learned that his horse had run away. A neighbor came by, saying, "What bad luck that you lost your valuable horse!"

The peasant replied, "Bad luck, good luck—who knows?"

Amazingly, the next day his horse returned, followed by a dozen wild horses. This time the neighbor came, saying, "What good luck that your horse would run away and return with a dozen horses! You are now a wealthy man."

Again, the peasant replied, "Good luck, bad luck—who knows?"

The next day the peasant's son broke his leg trying to break one of the wild horses. The neighbor consoled the father: "What bad luck that your son broke his leg and cannot work!"

The peasant responded, "Bad luck, good luck—who knows?"

Twenty-four hours later the army came through conscripting every young male into military service. The only exception was the peasant's son. He was excused because his leg was broken and he could not fight.

Again, the neighbor came by offering congratulations: "What good luck! Your son avoided military conscription because of his broken leg."

Ultimately, only God knows what is harmful and what is helpful; what is evil and what is good. God can transform lead into gold; pain into gain. We must learn not to be too quick to prejudge events. We must learn, too, that God can convert bad into good.

Reflect on the Scripture passage cited above. It is a statement made by Joseph, who was beaten by his brothers, thrown into a well, and left for dead. When the brothers realized that Joseph might still be alive, they returned to retrieve his body and sold him as a slave, thus profiting from their abuse. Even through those extreme circumstances, God made it possible for Joseph to emerge triumphantly as the prime minister of Egypt.

Be encouraged, therefore, because the same spiritual principle applies to those of us who have been bruised and battered at the hands of others. God's power can transform the lead in our lives into gold. God has the power and the will to make good come out of evil.

PRAYER

Eternal God, help me to trust you with my memories and my thoughts. Deepen my faith in your power to transform hurting into healing, bad into good, weakness into strength. Amen.

AFFIRMATIONS

I affirm the wisdom of God.

I affirm the power of God.

I affirm the creativity of God working in my life.

REFLECTION

God has reasons for everything that comes to pass.

Placid Riccardi

WEDNESDAY
Pushing Back the Darkness

We are in darkness now,
but the LORD will give us light.
Micah 7:8

Every person experiences a time when life is a struggle to push back the darkness.

- A man loses his job.

- A woman loses her husband.

- A child loses her health.

- Another man loses control over alcohol.

- Another woman loses the battle with drug abuse.

- Another child loses emotional stability.

If we expect our life journey to be always smooth, unobstructed, and comfortable, we are not realists. The people of faith whose journeys are recorded in the Bible frequently experienced dark periods in their lives. Many of the most saintly people in history had dark nights of the soul.

When the darkness descends upon us, we must remember—carefully and deliberately—the many promises in Scripture that God is with us in the darkness as surely as he is with us in the light. The movement from fear to faith means waiting and trusting God's light to break in upon our darkness.

PRAYER

Most merciful God, in my dark times help me to be patient. Remind me that your light can and will penetrate the deepest darkness. Amen.

AFFIRMATIONS

With God's help, I am moving through the darkness.

With God's help, I can handle this period of darkness.

With God's help, I am pushing back my darkness.

REFLECTION

When we are unable, God is able; when we feel insufficient, God is always sufficient; when we are filled with fear, God is always near.

William Arthur Ward

THURSDAY
The Importance of Acting "As If"

Even if I go through the deepest darkness,
I will not be afraid, LORD,
for you are with me.
Your shepherd's rod
and staff protect me.
Psalm 23:4

In his book *Tigers in the Dark*, Thomas Butts describes the time when all the electricity went out at a Barnum and Bailey circus. For a few moments, all the spectators and circus performers were in total darkness. In the greatest danger, however, was the animal trainer, who had just started his act in the tiger cage.

To the relief of all present, when the lights came on, the trainer was still alive. Later he was interviewed by television and newspaper reporters, who asked, "How did you feel in that cage with all those big cats in the dark? When they could see you and you couldn't see them?" The trainer responded, "The animals didn't know I couldn't see them, so I just cracked my whip and shouted commands."

We can take a valuable life lesson from that story. When we find ourselves in the dark, acting "as if" can be an effective way of pushing back the darkness. Like the animal trainer, acting "as if" can give us command of the situation. Acting "as if" is a faith posture that can link us to God, who is always with us in the darkness.

PRAYER

Loving God, do not allow me to become frightened and terrorized by the darkness. Strengthen and empower me to face darkness with courage, dignity, and faith, always knowing that you are present. Amen.

AFFIRMATIONS

I have power to control the darkness.

I relax and trust God to help me deal with descending darkness.

I have nothing to fear, because God is near.

REFLECTION

When our days become dreary with low-hovering clouds, and our nights become darker than a thousand midnights, let us remember that there is a great benign power in the universe whose name is God and who is able to make a way out of no way, and transform dark yesterdays into bright tomorrows.

Dr. Martin Luther King, Jr.

FRIDAY
Ten Commandments for Living

"Love your neighbor as you love yourself."
Matthew 22:39

In today's passage, Jesus reminds us that the second greatest commandment (after complete love for God) is to love our neighbors as we love ourselves. It should be noted that Jesus assumes we will *(and should)* love ourselves. In fact, psychologists observe that if we do not love ourselves, it is nearly impossible to truly love another person. The transition from fear to faith is dependent upon our ability to risk loving others as well as ourselves. Here are ten commandments for increasing love of self and love for others:

1. You shall concentrate on your good qualities. Admire and appreciate what is best in you. Thank God for those gifts.

2. You shall face all problems honestly, directly, and promptly. Do whatever it takes to improve your life.

3. You shall be a source of inspiration, hope, and courage for others who come in contact with you.

4. You shall be kind to all people, seeking out their good qualities and not their faults.

5. You shall widen your mercy and narrow your judgment when it comes to yourself and to others.

6. You shall look upon your "failures" as learning experiences and lessons in living. Looking at them carefully will help you avoid repeating mistakes.

7. You shall reduce worry and anxiety in your life by recalling your successes rather than your shortcomings.

8. You shall remember that the movement toward wholeness is two steps forward and one step backward. Therefore, don't be discouraged when you experience a setback.

9. You shall commit some of your time and talent to helping other people on a regular basis.

10. You shall remember that people, not things, are the most important gifts in life.

PRAYER

On this journey of life, O God, be my companion and guide. Day by day, teach me how to love you, to love others, to love myself. Wherever I am in my journey between birth and death, grant me your peace and your presence. Amen.

AFFIRMATIONS

I have nothing to fear in loving myself.

I have nothing to fear in loving others.

I am powerful, and I am loving.

REFLECTION

It is to those who have the most need that we ought to show our love more especially.

Saint Francis de Sales

SATURDAY
God's Unlimited Power

"This is impossible for man, but for God everything is possible."
Matthew 19:26

We must always remember that God can heal our memories and pains. Although we may be convinced that it is impossible to find relief from past traumas, Jesus forcefully declares that for God everything is possible. To help with the movement from fear to faith, perhaps this story from a recent issue of *American Health* magazine can provide insight and motivation.

Hans Poulsen is a forty-five-year-old songwriter from Sydney, Australia, who was diagnosed with testicular cancer. He agreed to surgery but declined further therapy. The doctors told him that even with ongoing therapy his prognosis was grim.

"I don't remember exactly how much time the doctors gave me," says Poulson. "What I do recall vividly is one doctor saying that if I were in a horse race, he certainly wouldn't bet on me."

Poulson's doctors wanted him to follow surgery with both radiation and chemotherapy. Poulson refused. Instead, he began a personal process of mental imagery and invited people of faith to pray for his recovery. A year later, Poulson was back in the hospital after collapsing while onstage at a concert in California. This time, the doctors found that the cancer had spread to other parts of his body.

"He was given up for dead," says Poulsen's physician, Dr. Richard Ingrasci, head of the Wellsprings Center for Life Enhancement, a nonprofit cancer support group in Watertown, Massachusetts. "He had tumors as big as baseballs in his lungs, tumors pressing on both kidneys, and cancer in his lymph system." Finally, the psychiatrist persuaded Poulson to take *one* chemotherapy treatment, thinking it might tip the balance in his favor.

The results of that treatment are legendary in the corridors of Mount Auburn Hospital in Boston, where Poulsen was being treated. "His oncologist ran down the corridor yelling, 'His tumors are disappearing before my eyes! It's a miracle!'" recalls Dr. Ingrasci.

Eight years later, Poulsen's cancer was in complete remission. Poulsen credits both traditional medicine and faith. "One could not have worked without the other," he says.

PRAYER

May the healing love of God come upon me and fill me, making me whole in body, mind, and spirit. Amen.

AFFIRMATIONS

I give thanks for divine restoration.

The light of God within me produces perfect results.

The love of God is creating miracles in my life.

REFLECTION

Put on your jumping shoes, and jump into the heart of God.
                                            Meister Eckhart

SUNDAY

The Stabilizing
Influence of Friends

People learn from one another, just as iron sharpens iron.
Proverbs 27:17

Although some individuals have hurt us badly, we must never turn away completely from people. We must allow ourselves to be nurtured by good friends. Those who decline closeness deprive themselves of emotional stability and clarity of perception. In isolation, our problems become greatly magnified.

However, a good friend can provide healthy balance and perspective. By sharing our thoughts with a trusted friend, we will have a more realistic sense of the events that shape our lives. On the other hand, in isolation,

- a minor setback may be viewed as a major catastrophe

- abuse by significant adults from the past can leave us convinced that we are unworthy of anyone's love and friendship

- today's darkness and depression can seem to be a permanent condition.

We can reduce and eliminate these dangerous and wrong perceptions by confiding in another person who will help us draw healthier conclusions about our lives. That is the wisdom contained in today's text: *People learn from one another, just as iron sharpens iron.*

PRAYER

Loving and kind God, although I have been hurt by some people in my past, lead me now to healthy friends. Help me resist the temptation to withdraw and live in isolation from others. Guide me and bless me in the formation of new friendships. Amen.

AFFIRMATIONS

I acknowledge my need for a good friend.

I am open to forming healthy friendships.

I am open to honest sharing.

REFLECTION

Friendship is a sheltering tree.

Samuel Taylor Coleridge

MONDAY

When Friends Are More Important Than Family

Some friends are more loyal than brothers.
Proverbs 18:24

Redwoods are the world's tallest living trees. Found along the West Coast from southwest Oregon to central California, these giant trees often tower over three hundred feet.

With such height, one would think the tree would require deep roots. Yet redwoods have a very shallow root system, carefully designed to capture as much surface moisture as possible. The roots spread out in all directions, and as a result, all the roots of all the trees in a redwood grove become intertwined. They are locked together for mutual protection and support. When a fierce wind blows or a strong storm strikes, all the trees sustain one another. That is why one almost never sees a redwood tree standing alone. They need one another to survive.

This lesson from the redwood tree raises an important question about our family of origin. Does our family of origin provide us with the support we need? Do we feel good when we are with family of origin members? Does our family of origin sustain and strengthen us?

If the answer to such questions is a resounding no, then we need to consider relating to a family of choice—friends who will provide us with the love, affirmation, and acceptance we all need. As with the California redwoods, our "real" family is made up of people emotionally locked together to provide support and mutual strength. When fierce winds and strong storms of life blow our way, it is our family of choice that provides us with safe refuge.

PRAYER

Gracious Lord, empower me to turn away from people who hurt me. Help me recognize and turn toward my true family—people who affirm and accept, strengthen and support me. Amen.

AFFIRMATIONS

I am grateful for the healing presence of friends.

I am successfully creating a healthy family of choice.

God is blessing me with good friends.

REFLECTION

Fate chooses our relatives. We choose our friends.

Jacques Bossuet

TUESDAY
Trusting Others Again

I was eyes for the blind,
and feet for the lame.
Job 29:15

A woman vividly recalls an important lesson learned as a child living in Alaska.

At the time, her family had the task of turning Alaskan wilderness into farmland. The children were given the job of clearing off charred logs from forest fires of earlier years. They would gather the logs and place them into huge piles for burning.

One day as they watched the fires glowing, a single log rolled away from the glowing mass. For a few minutes it continued to glow; but gradually it grew less and less red, finally turning black. As they all watched the log, the father said, "This reminds me of a lesson about people. See what happens when a stick tries to burn alone? It's the same with a person. We all glow more brightly when we link up with others, when we encourage one another."

That lesson, so true, is especially applicable to those dealing with life's hurts. We all need friends, not just for good times but in bad times as well. Even though we have been hurt by those closest to us, it is always a mistake to pull away. We need one another to balance life. Job puts it eloquently in today's Scripture passage. Friends can become our eyes when we cannot see clearly and our feet when we are too lame to walk.

PRAYER

Most merciful God, let me not lose faith in other people. Continue to teach me the importance of friendship. Send good people into my life and let me be good for them as well. Amen.

AFFIRMATIONS

I recognize others as loving, kind people.

I release all mechanisms for blocking people out of my life.

I accept love freely and with gratitude.

REFLECTION

Friendship is a thing most necessary to life.

Aristotle

WEDNESDAY
Trusting God to Guide Us

...this is God,
our God forever and ever.
He will be our guide forever.
Psalm 48:14
(*New Revised Standard Version*)

There is never a time in our lives when God is not seeking to gently guide us. A good example is former Olympic skier Jimmie Huega. In 1970 he was diagnosed with multiple sclerosis (MS). At that time, the standard medical wisdom was that MS patients should live quiet, nonphysical lives. Physicians believed that engaging in sports and any other exercise would further weaken the body, allowing MS to spread more rapidly.

Determined to make the best of a bad situation, Huega reluctantly accepted the prescription to lead a quiet life. However, after four inactive years he felt worse, not better. Fearing further physical, mental, and spiritual deterioration, Huega felt led to disregard the advice to take it easy.

As a result, he devised his own treatment plan. "One in which I, not the disease, took charge," he says. Huega embarked on a vigorous exercise program that included strengthening exercises such as cycling (twelve hundred miles the first year) and swimming five hundred laps daily.

Although his doctors were hesitant to endorse his plan, Huega acted on his intuition. Within a few months he was healthier and happier than he had been in four years. He married, and his doctors were surprised when he fathered a child, since this is normally difficult for men with MS. Huega and his wife now have two children.

Today Huega shares his "reanimation" program with other MS sufferers. Over the years he has urged experts to reconsider the role of exercise in illness. Subsequent studies confirm what Huega experienced: rather than speeding deterioration, exercise can strengthen and energize MS patients, physically and emotionally.

The lesson from Jimmie Huega is this: we must learn to listen to our intuition. The "voice" that comes from deep within is often God calling and guiding us to a healthier place.

PRAYER

Loving God, help me to sense your leading in my life. Help me respond with faith and trust. Amen.

AFFIRMATIONS

I am filled with God's vibrant, living force.

I am filled with God's beauty, strength, and light.

I am filled with God's power for living.

REFLECTION

There is nothing but God's grace.
We walk upon it;
we breathe it;
we live and die by it;
it makes the nails and axles of the universe.

Robert Louis Stevenson

THURSDAY
The Importance of Self-Care

"You have six days in which to do your work,
but the seventh day is a day of rest...."
Exodus 20:9-10

This, the third of the ten commandments, is especially important for those working to heal the inner child. Most survivors of childhood abuse tend to become caregivers rather than care receivers. It is easy to focus upon the needs of others while neglecting ourselves. Yet in the Scriptures we are reminded of the importance of self-care. For "six days" we are permitted to work and take care of others, but the "seventh day" must be a day of rest. That "seventh day" is an invitation and opportunity to engage in personal renewal and self-care. Here are some ways to begin providing self-care.

- Learn to say no to the many demands for your support and time.

- Learn to identify your needs and ask others to help meet your needs.

- Do something just for yourself. Take a class, go on a trip, start a relaxing hobby.

- Remind yourself that you do not have to be in the presence of people who mistreat you.

- Begin to weed out people who put you down and generally make you feel worse about yourself.

- Start surrounding yourself with people who are supportive, loyal, and truly loving.

By following these suggestions and adding some ideas of your own, you will become your own nurturing parent. You will begin giving yourself the care you missed as a child, and you will raise your self-esteem.

PRAYER

Eternal and holy God, thank you for stressing the importance of a Sabbath day for rest, renewal, and refreshment. Help me take seriously the importance of self-care. Help me become whole in body, in mind, and in spirit. Amen.

AFFIRMATIONS

I attract healthy, loving people into my life.

I affirm my needs and seek to have them filled.

I am opening up to the best within me.

REFLECTION

Keep a green tree in your heart, and perhaps a singing bird will come.

Chinese proverb

FRIDAY
Say Yes to Yourself

"...you are precious to me...
I love you and give you honor."
Isaiah 43:4

Sadly, one of the realities of inner-child abuse is a severely damaged self-image. Symptoms include

- feeling ugly inside,

- feeling worthless and inadequate

- believing that you are the source of other people's problems

- feeling like a loser in life, no matter what accomplishments you have made

- feeling trapped, helpless, and hopeless.

When such thoughts manifest themselves, it can be extremely helpful to remind yourself of God's view: *"You are precious to me...I love you and give you honor."* Use that statement to reorient your thinking about yourself. Try saying the following to yourself: *Because I am precious and honored and loved by God, I will*

- praise and compliment myself

- give myself credit for being a survivor

- identify and appreciate my accomplishments

- encourage myself when I feel frightened, intimidated, or weak

- make it a habit to recall the best in myself—my courage, honesty, and integrity.

PRAYER

Almighty and gentle God, teach me to value myself as you value me. Give me compassion for myself, and help me believe you do love, honor, and care for me. Amen.

AFFIRMATIONS

The all-powerful God knows me and loves me.

God gives my life meaning and purpose.

With God, I have the power to bring dignity into my life.

REFLECTION

Grace strikes us when we are in great pain and restlessness. It strikes us when we walk through the dark valley of a meaningless and empty life. It strikes us when we feel that our separation is deeper than usual.

Paul Tillich

SATURDAY
Exercising Freedom of Choice

…we win the victory over the world by means of our faith.
1 John 5:4

We must never allow ourselves to believe the lie that we are the only ones who suffer; that others live lives free of pain. Sooner or later, intense suffering invades every life. It may take the form of

- an illness

- a tragic accident

- the death of a beloved child or spouse or friend

- a major depression

- a break in an important relationship

- an awareness of hurt inflicted in the distant past.

Sometimes we are hit with several problems at once. While we do not have control over painful events that come our way, we do have freedom in how we respond to affliction. We can choose to respond negatively or positively, in faith or in fear. Always, the choice is ours.

Today's Scripture reminds us that we can "win victory over the world by means of our faith." This victory happens when we choose to move from tears to trust. We must learn to believe in ourselves and in our God, to believe that we are given abilities and graces to manage trauma and crisis.

Winning the victory means exercising our freedom of choice. When we choose to respond creatively to suffering,

- we will grow in self-understanding

- we will grow in sensitivity to others

- we will grow in our understanding and experience of God.

Although it is true that suffering colors our lives, we have the right to choose the color. It is God's desire that each of us develops rich and beautiful hues in our lives as we face hurt and pain with trust.

PRAYER

Dear God, help me to be fearless in facing my pains, give me the heart to conquer my hurts, grant me the patience to forge good out of the pain that has come into my life. Amen.

AFFIRMATIONS

The Christ within strengthens me.
The Christ within guides me.
The Christ within heals me.

REFLECTION

If you always do what you've always done, you'll always get what you've always gotten.

Alan Cohen

SUNDAY
Choose Your Attitude

"I am now giving you the choice between life and death....Choose life."
Deuteronomy 30:19

Several years ago, a North American couple living in India gave birth to their first child. When the little boy was only six months old, he became ill and died. Of course, his parents' grief was deep and dark. Upon learning of their loss, an elderly Indian gentleman came to bring them comfort. With great sensitivity and wisdom he said:

A tragedy like this is like being plunged into boiling water. If you are an egg, your affliction will make you hard-boiled and unresponsive. If you are a potato, you will emerge soft and pliable, resilient and adaptable. Which do you want to be?

There are times when events come into our lives over which we have no control. Yet we can decide to choose our attitude toward those events. And the choices are clear: we can become bitter or better,
cold or warm,
hard or soft,
angry or accepting,
healthy or unhealthy.
Always, there is a choice. The Bible urges us to choose life, not death.

PRAYER

Loving God, although painful events have been forced upon me, I ask you to help me respond wisely and with faith. Help me choose the right attitudes and emerge a stronger, healthier person. Amen.

AFFIRMATIONS

Today I am choosing healthy attitudes.

Today I will settle down and see this through.

Today I will say yes to my life.

REFLECTION

Things don't change; you change your way of looking, that's all.

Carlos Castaneda

MONDAY
Control Your Destiny

"Be determined and confident. Do not be afraid...."
Deuteronomy 31:6

When Barbara Hansen was nineteen years old, she was critically injured in an automobile accident. Although she survived the wreck, she has used a wheelchair ever since. Today she is fifty-six, a professor of English at Raymond Walters College, University of Cincinnati, and author of *Picking Up the Pieces: Healing Ourselves After Personal Loss.*

It is worth noting that Hansen has been in a wheelchair for the last thirty-seven years. During most of that period, there was not today's openness about people with disabilities. Most buildings did not have wheelchair access ramps; many schools and employers would not give people in wheelchairs opportunities to learn and work. In spite of various personal and social obstacles, Hansen remained determined and confident to reclaim and rebuild her life. Now, she says:

> I was surprised at how many people who, when loss hit them, had nothing to fall back on. They thought they were leaves in the wind, blown about by circumstances over which they had no control. It's amazing how much we do control our own destiny. "We have no control over the circumstances that come into our lives, but I know in my own life that circumstances aren't as important as the attitudes that I take to those circumstances."

Like Barbara Hansen, the Bible reminds us that we can control our destiny when we choose our attitude. For that reason, the biblical writer declares: "*Be determined and confident. Do not be afraid.*"

PRAYER

Eternal and loving God, remind me that you have not abandoned me in this world; that you are present in every event of my life. Help me to trust you and move forward with determination and confidence. Amen.

AFFIRMATIONS

My God is an unfailing source of strength and courage.

I am now ready to accept God's help.

I am allowing courage to build in me.

REFLECTION

As a man thinketh so is he, and as a man chooseth, so is he.
Ralph Waldo Emerson

TUESDAY
Living Victoriously in Spite of Hardship

You do yourself a favor when you are kind.
Proverbs 11:17

One of the signs that we are moving from feeling like victims to functioning as victors in life lies in our ability to be kind. Kindness is always a virtue of emotionally, strong healthy people. In spite of their own hardships, they touch others with kindness.

While Averell Harriman was ambassador to the Soviet Union from 1943 to 1946, he was followed everywhere by the Soviet secret police. One weekend he was invited to visit a British diplomat at his country retreat. The house was accessible only by a four-wheel-drive vehicle. Considerately, Harriman warned his followers of that fact.

Nevertheless, the secret police followed Harriman's jeep in their customary sedan, which soon became hopelessly bogged down. One of the Soviet agents left the car to follow Harriman on foot. With resolute kindness, Harriman slowed down to allow the walker to keep up. Soon Harriman, concerned that the agent would freeze to death before they reached their destination, offered him a ride, promising he would tell no one about the incident. The man accepted. As a result, the ambassador and the Soviet secret-police agent rode together for the rest of the journey.

PRAYER

Eternal and loving God, help me to take the focus off myself by performing acts of kindness and compassion to others. Open my eyes that I may see and hear the needs of other hurting people. Amen.

AFFIRMATIONS

Today I will be the cup of strength for suffering souls.

Today I will inspire others with joy and gladness.

Today I will let God's love flow freely
through me and on to others.

REFLECTION

Let me be a little kinder.

Edgar Albert Guest

WEDNESDAY
Doing the Work

"But now don't be discouraged, any of you.
Do the work, for I am with you."
Haggai 2:4

This verse conveys two important thoughts. First, the tasks of recovery and of rebuilding our lives take work. Second, as we expend the energy to do that work, God promises to be present and bless our efforts.

There is no quick fix to the abuse of the inner child. It takes hard, disciplined work. The work of reclaiming our lives often means

- joining a regular support group

- going for therapy

- reading literature about abuse and recovery

- taking classes dealing with abuse issues

- confiding in trusted friends

- releasing suppressed emotions

- detaching from our family of origin

- confronting abusers.

Even though these tasks are difficult and can be discouraging, we must remember God's promise to bless our efforts. Those who have done the work of recovery say the gains far outweigh the pains. They say that their anger, fear, guilt, pain, and self-loathing gave way to self-discovery, self-forgiveness, self-care, self-acceptance, and a welcome intimacy in relationships.

PRAYER

Gracious God, help me to face my past honestly and openly. Empower me to do the work necessary for reclaiming my life. Amen.

AFFIRMATIONS

I am a responsible person.

I am strong enough to face my fears.

I have the power to bring dignity into my life.

REFLECTION

Why not upset the apple cart? If you don't, the apples will rot anyway.

Frank A. Clark

THURSDAY
The Power of Self-Perception

You give me strength for the battle....
2 Samuel 22:40

When fourteen-year-old Shane Gould was on her way to becoming a champion swimmer, a reporter asked the Australian girl how she thought she would do at a swim meet here in the United States. Shane replied, "I have a feeling there will be a world record today." She went on to set two world records in the one-hundred- and two-hundred-meter freestyle events.

Later Gould was asked how she thought she would fare in the more grueling four-hundred-meter event. Smiling, Shane replied, "I get stronger every race, and besides, my parents said they'd take me to Disneyland if I win, and we're leaving tomorrow!" She left for Disneyland holding three world records.

At the age of sixteen, Shane Gould held five world records and became one of the greatest swimmers of all time. At the 1972 Olympics, she won three gold medals. Fortunately for Gould, she understood the power of self-perception.

How do you see yourself? Do you see yourself as capable, confident, strong, and powerful? Or do you see yourself as a needy, timid, hesitant, and even cringing person? If you answer affirmatively to the latter, then reflect upon today's biblical passage from the Second Book of Samuel. It is a reminder that God gives all of us the strength and power we need to deal with every life event. Knowing that, we should begin to perceive ourselves as marathon winners in the contests of life. By the grace of God, we can be victors and not victims.

PRAYER

Eternal and loving God, help me to view myself more positively. Remind me that I am created in the image of God; that you provide me with strength to meet and manage every situation. Amen.

AFFIRMATIONS

I am taking action.

I am reclaiming my power.

I am now taking control of my life.

REFLECTION

First, say to yourself what you would be, and then do what you have to do.

Epictetus

FRIDAY
Deciding to Fight

"Be strong and don't be afraid!
God is coming to your rescue."
Isaiah 35:4

"I had a decision to make. I could either lie in my hospital bed feeling sorry for myself or fight to get better. I decided to fight." Those statements were made by twenty-nine-year-old Barbara Cross. In April 1990 she became extremely ill and was diagnosed with multiple sclerosis (MS).

Knowing that many of those afflicted with this degenerative disease of the central nervous system become paralyzed, Cross was initially in despair. "Picturing myself in a wheelchair," she says, "I lay in the hospital feeling as if my future had been stripped away."

After the initial shock, Cross felt the energy to fight back and implemented a plan to take control of her life. The plan included attending MS support-group meetings, learning about the disease, and meeting people who struggled with symptoms far worse than hers. Their courage gave Cross more strength to carry on. In addition, Cross began an exercise program, eventually rejoining her aerobics class.

When faced with personal trauma, some people remain paralyzed by fear. Others simply give up hope and life. However, healthy individuals will choose to stand firm and fight back in any way they can.

Often the decision to face the trauma is made easier when

we know that "God is coming to our rescue." Today's Scripture reminds us that we are not left to be soloists in the universe but that God is present with helping power. Sometimes the help God gives is like that given to Barbara Cross: an infusion of energy and the will to fight back.

PRAYER

Eternal and loving God, renew my heart, fortify my will, strengthen my desires, purify my mind, cleanse my spirit through Jesus Christ, my Lord. Amen.

AFFIRMATIONS

I will press forward.

I will not be defeated.

I will never, never give up.

REFLECTION

Hope means hoping when things are hopeless, or it is no virtue at all. It is only when everything is hopeless that hope begins to be a strength.

G.K. Chesterton

SATURDAY

Determination Plus Dedication Produces Distinction

Being lazy will make you poor,
but hard work will make you rich.
Proverbs 10:4

The author of Proverbs reminds us that the path to personal and professional success always involves hard work. Those who are too "lazy" and unmotivated to work at recovery from inner-child abuse will remain "poor." On the other hand, those who work hard at overcoming past pain will become "rich." Determination plus dedication always produces men and women of distinction.

An inspiring example is Terry King, blinded after a shell burst in his face while training for combat in Vietnam. Even though he could not see, King loved the water and always longed for a cabin cruiser. Unable to afford one, he decided to build one himself. But how could a blind man build a boat?

After committing himself to the project, King found a volunteer from the Blind Service Association, Inc., who was willing to tape-record a book on boat building. By listening to the tapes, King built a thirty-three-foot cabin cruiser in his backyard. Though he would always need someone to pilot it, he was thrilled, because building the boat was the "biggest challenge I could meet."

Terry King is an excellent example of the truth that dedication plus determination produces distinction. Terry King is the type of person the writer of Proverbs had in mind: *"Being lazy will make you poor, but hard work will make you rich."*

PRAYER

Dear God, deepen my determination and dedication to recovery. Bless my hard work with the riches of joy and peace, I pray through Jesus Christ, my Lord. Amen.

AFFIRMATIONS

God's love and light are working in my life right now.

God is showing the way now.

The power of God creates a miracle in my life here and now.

REFLECTION

People go about their tasks without weariness if they have a goal and a belief in what they are doing.

Dr. Arnold Hutschnecker

SUNDAY
Getting Grief Relief

*He changed deserts into pools of water
and dry land into flowing springs.*
Psalm 107:35

Because the inner child has been bruised and battered, there will be "dry" spells in living. Often these are characterized by feelings of depression, darkness, and even despair. Yet this Scripture passage declares that God can refresh a dry spirit. This transformation can take place more easily when we open ourselves to God's healing action.

Here are ten ways to establish an openness before God.

1. Read and reread the Scriptures on God's loving intent toward you. Especially valuable are Psalm 23, Luke 4:18-19, and Philippians 4:4-20.

2. Find a quiet place and make some time to pray and meditate.

3. Ask God to show you the next step in your emotional and spiritual growth. Then take that step.

4. Conduct an examination of conscience. Ask yourself some honest questions. Are you overly negative about your life? Are you guilty of seeing only problems and not possibilities? Are your thoughts healthy or unhealthy?

5. Write out a "dream" list. What would you like to have

happen in your life this year, next year, in five years? Keep this list nearby. Review it and update it periodically.

6. Share your burden with a trusted friend.

7. Listen to some children's music or favorite hymns.

8. Send a note of encouragement to someone who needs a lift.

9. Write a letter of appreciation to someone who helped you.

10. Expand your love by sharing it with someone. Visit a hospital, a hospice, a shelter.

PRAYER

Merciful God, thank you for the promise of renewal and refreshment. During my dry times, help me to trust and wait patiently for you. Amen.

AFFIRMATIONS

God's love is working perfectly in my life.

God is showing me the way to abundant living.

God's light is flooding my path now.

REFLECTION

I am oppressed by the uncertainty of my future, but I cherish the lively hope of seeing my dreams fulfilled, because the Lord cannot place thoughts and desires in a person's soul and not really intend to fulfill them.

Padre Pio

MONDAY

Transforming Sadness Into Gladness

"…your sadness will turn into gladness."
John 16:20

A woman tells how she transformed sorrow one day. In the preceding year, she had lost four relatives, all to untimely deaths. Feeling deep sorrow after her husband left for work one morning, she was gazing out the window and reflecting on the short lives of her loved ones. Suddenly, she was aware of how fortunate she was to have this day ahead of her. A powerful idea came into her mind: *What would each of my loved ones do with just one more day to live?*

She decided to live that day doing what each of her loved ones would have done.

- She began baking chocolate chip cookies to welcome a new neighbor, as her mother-in-law would have done.

- She donated used clothing to a needy organization, as her brother would have done.

- She phoned a friend she had lost touch with, as her sister-in-law would have done.

- She smiled a lot that day, as her grandchild would have done.

With that inspiration guiding her, the woman reports, sorrow turned to joy as she tried to help others in memory of her loved ones.

PRAYER

Loving God, give me the insight to see the pain of others, the sensitivity to feel the pain of others, and the strength to relieve the pain of others. Amen.

AFFIRMATIONS

Today I am aware that life is hard for everyone.

Today I am aware that others suffer as well.

Today I will extend special kindness and consideration to others.

REFLECTION

God gave us a memory that we might have roses in December.

James M. Barrie

TUESDAY
The Courage to Confront Our Pain

"Be determined and confident, and don't be afraid....
We have more power on our side...."
2 Chronicles 32:7

Lions travel in a group called a pride. There is always a king, or leader, the strongest and most courageous lion. He remains king of the pride only as long as he is physically able to hold his position over the younger lions.

When the king lion ages and weakens, he is replaced. By then, the old king may not have any teeth left and only a few claws. His hair is diminishing, and he usually has arthritis.

Nevertheless, the old lion plays an important role in the pride. On hunts, he stands alone in a clearing, while the other lions hide in the bushes. When a deer comes into the clearing, it sees the old king, who gives out a mighty roar.

This roar scares the deer so badly that it runs as fast as it can in the opposite direction, right into the waiting jaws of the young lions, who quickly kill the prey. Ironically, if the deer had run toward the roar, it would have escaped harm. All the old, toothless, arthritic lion could have done to the deer was chase it briefly before giving up.

The lesson for those dealing with abuse of the inner child is this: Don't run away from the "roar" of hurt and rejection. Face the loss, the pain, and the fear. Face them with courage, dignity, and patience. This is the only way to make the transition from pain to peace.

PRAYER

Loving God, I am no longer willing to live with my pain. I am no longer willing to avoid it, deny it, suppress it, or ignore it. Give me courage to face my pain creatively. Amen.

AFFIRMATIONS

I am willing to be happy.

I am willing to receive the best in life.

I accept all my feelings as important parts of myself.

REFLECTION

Some people run away from grief, go on world cruises, or move to another town. But they do not escape. The memories, unbidden, spring into their minds, scattered perhaps over the years. There is something to be said for facing them all deliberately and straightaway.

Sheldon Vanauken

WEDNESDAY
Changing Internalized Messages

See how much the Father has loved us!
1 John 3:1

Sometimes healing of the inner child is impeded by negative internal messages.

- I don't deserve anything better.

- Everything is my fault.

- I hate myself.

- I am not worthy of love and respect.

- I'll never feel different. I am a bad person.

- I can never change.

- It's hopeless.

These negative internal messages have their origin in childhood. Every abused child quickly learns this false message: *I am not worthy of protection or love.* In turn, that signal leads to low self-esteem.

Yet internalized negative messages can and must be changed. This is essential for healing and making the transition from pain to peace. Whenever a negative internal message surfaces in your mind, try to counterbalance it immediately by personalizing and reciting this passage from the First Letter of John: *See how much the Father loves me!*

If this exercise seems artificial at first, remind yourself that the singular message that rings and radiates throughout the entire Bible is the fact that God loves, values, respects, and honors you.

PRAYER

Merciful God, help me to believe in your love for me. And let your love so transform me that I will be a living witness to your goodness. Amen.

AFFIRMATIONS

Because of God's love for me, I celebrate myself.

Because of God's love for me, I value myself.

Because of God's love for me, I honor myself.

REFLECTION

Let nothing dismay me.
God made me.
God loves me and keeps me,
      gives comfort and grace for every need
      at every moment,
      in and around me,
      within me.
Thanks be to God.

George Appleton

THURSDAY
Failure Is Never Total

"And now I make all things new!"
Revelation 21:5

Those whose inner child was abused need to find ways to liberate themselves from the tyranny of feeling like failures in life. Such thoughts need to be banished from the mind. They must never be allowed to control you. Whenever feelings of failure begin to oppress you, talk back to them. Here are some suggestions.

- *Failure is no disgrace.* I will keep on trying until things begin to change. At least I have the health to try new things.

- *Failure can be fruitful.* I will look at all my failures, shortcomings, and mistakes to see what I can learn from them. Failures can be invaluable life lessons.

- *Failure is simply the sign of my humanness.* I'm not perfect. No one is. I'm human, and all human beings make mistakes and experience failures and setbacks.

- *Failure is never final.* There is always another chapter to be written for my life. Learning from the past, I can forge a better, brighter future for myself.

- *Failure is never total.* Today's verse from the Book of Revelation is a promise that God is the One who can make all things new. My God can take the fractured, broken lives of people and recreate them.

- *Failure is just one small aspect of my life.* Although I have my share of failures, I also have many positive strengths. (Recite a list of good things about yourself: your dedication, your compassion, your discipline, your academic achievements, and so forth.)

- *Failure is a motivator.* Whenever I fail, I review what happened and reevaluate my goals. I transform failure into a motivating force, propelling me to do differently and better next time—and there is always a next time.

PRAYER

Loving and merciful God, liberate me from the tyranny of negative feelings. Free me from being too harsh with myself, and help me trust your power to recreate my life. Amen.

AFFIRMATIONS

I am a beautiful person with much to contribute to those around me.

I respect who I am.

I am learning from all of life's experiences.

REFLECTION

There is much to be said for failure. It is more interesting than success.

Max Beerbohm

FRIDAY
Moving Forward One Step at a Time

"My grace is all you need...."
2 Corinthians 12:9

In today's Scripture text, we read Saint Paul's grand declaration that God's strength is our strength. This means that there is no difficulty that cannot be overcome and no problem that is insurmountable. One way to cooperate with God's spirit is to take the next step on faith. We all must cross our mountains and valleys one step at a time. Along the journey, we will discover God's power working on our behalf.

Sixteen years ago Pam Lontos was unemployed and forty pounds overweight. "I was afraid of everything," she says. "Nothing was going my way."

One day in 1976, on impulse, the thirty-one-year-old woman joined a health club. She began listening to motivational tapes as well. Her mind began working, thinking, and dreaming. As her appearance improved, so did her self-esteem. "I was still plagued with fear of failure, but I decided I had to take steps toward a career goal," she recalls.

Lontos asked the club's owner for a job selling memberships. Within a few months she was the club's top salesperson. After two years that experience led to a better job in advertising sales with Dallas's lowest rated radio station. After Lontos arrived, sales began to soar.

Her impressive record was quickly noted by the station's owners, Shamrock Broadcasting. They promoted her to corporate vice president. "In three and a half years, I'd gone from an overweight housewife to an executive with a major entertainment company," she says proudly. "I did it by taking small steps. That's the only way I could overcome my fears of failing."

PRAYER

Holy and good God, thank you for the promise of your grace to help me. As I move forward, day by day, guide me, strengthen me, encourage me, and make me whole. Amen.

AFFIRMATIONS

Through God's grace, I dissolve all negative, limiting beliefs.

Through God's grace, I am letting go of all accumulated pain, guilt, and fear.

Through God's grace, I am moving toward wholeness and peace.

REFLECTION

We make the path by walking.

Robert Bly

SATURDAY
Pursuing Persistently

…let us run with determination the race that lies before us.
Hebrews 12:1

The journey from pain to peace must include a fierce determination on our part. It means we must pursue persistently the goal we have set for ourselves. Only as we do this can we achieve and enjoy victory.

Michael Blake, author of *Dances With Wolves,* won an Academy Award for the movie adaptation. He is extremely successful now, but less than ten years ago, he was homeless, living and sleeping in his car. Today he shuns the bestseller book tours in favor of speaking to children at libraries and schools.

Recently, Blake met with a group of homeless grade school children at a branch of the Brooklyn Public Library. "I told them if you stay committed, your dreams can come true. I'm living proof it it," he stated. "I left home at seventeen and had nothing but rejection for twenty-five years. I wrote more than twenty screenplays, but I never gave up."

Although the movement from pain to peace can be difficult and discouraging, our determination is what will make the vital difference.

PRAYER

Loving God, keep me strong so that I can continue the journey from pain to peace, from hurting to healing, from sadness to gladness. Amen.

AFFIRMATIONS

God strengthens me.

God empowers me.

God creates miracles in my life.

REFLECTION

There is no success without hardship.

Sophocles

SUNDAY

Choosing to Transform Painful Experiences

I will...make Trouble Valley a door of hope.
Hosea 2:15

Human beings are unique in that they can rise above suffering, tragedy, and deprivation. God provides every woman and man with the ability to renew, re-create, and begin again, regardless of what has happened to them. One of the advantages of adversity is that out of its pain people often rise, expand, grow, and achieve.

Consider the example of Robert Howard Allen. When he first arrived at Bethel College in McKenzie, Tennessee, he was thirty-two, with unkempt hair and a tattered sweater held together by safety pins. The young man had never been in school and had spent most of his life in virtual isolation, with only elderly relatives for company. Yet his learning was impressive.

Robert's parents were divorced when he was only a few months old. Although he longs for contact with his father, he has never seen him. When he was six, Robert's mother left him to be raised by a grandfather, three great-aunts, and a great-uncle, all of whom lived in the same Tennessee backwoods house. An aunt, Bevie Jones, taught him to read, and his grandfather taught him to write. Robert, in turn, read the *King James Bible* to his blind Aunt Ida.

Beginning at age seven, Robert read thousands of books—from Donald Duck comics to Homer, James Joyce, and William Shakespeare. Hungry for more, he began to buy books at yard sales and by his early twenties had read more than two thousand volumes. "Books were my great comfort," he says. "They were my pastime and my playmates." Robert never rode a bicycle or went to a movie. At age thirty, he took a high school equivalency test and easily passed.

In 1984, after three years at Bethel, he graduated summa cum laude with a 3.92 grade-point average. And in 1991 Robert Howard Allen graduated from Vanderbilt University with a Ph.D. in English. He is currently a visiting lecturer at Murray State University in Kentucky.

PRAYER

Loving God, help me take my "trouble valley" and transform it into a "door of hope." Thank you for not abandoning me; thank you for your continuous care of me. Amen.

AFFIRMATIONS

I am asking and listening to God's guidance.

I am asking and receiving God's plan.

I am asking and responding to God's love.

REFLECTION

Adversity causes some men to break; others to break records.
                                        William Arthur Ward

MONDAY
Imposing Order on Our Living

"I will turn their darkness into light."
Isaiah 42:16

When the inner child has been bruised and battered, one of the lingering impacts is the feeling of emotional chaos and spiritual darkness. In this Old Testament passage, the prophet declares God's intention to turn "darkness into light." For this divine action to take place, however, there must also be human cooperation. One effective way to help this come about is to impose order on our lives.

This is a principle used by television personality Ed McMahon whenever he has had a difficult transition in his life. At age sixty-nine, McMahon having weathered many life challenges, faced another in his departure from *The Tonight Show* at Johnny Carson's retirement. McMahon advises:

> When it's time for a major change, the demands of daily life can get out of control. You may begin to daydream, worry, sleep late, eat improperly, or lose track of time. The result may be frustration and poor performance. To counter such tendencies, I focus on simple disciplines such as punctuality and preparation.

Ordeal can be transformed into fulfillment only when we exercise daily discipline and impose structure onto our living.

PRAYER

Merciful God, in the beginning, you created light in the darkness and imposed order upon chaos. I ask you to re-create these in my life. Help me cooperate with your healing actions upon my living. Amen.

AFFIRMATIONS

Today I choose light over darkness.

Today I choose faith over fear.

Today I choose order over chaos

REFLECTION

The way in which we accept our fate and all the suffering it entails, the way in which we take up our cross, gives ample opportunity—even under the most difficult circumstances—to add to a deeper meaning of life.

Viktor Frankl

T∪ESDAY
Acting on Opportunities

You have made many wonderful plans for us.
Psalm 40:5

In this passage, the Psalmist reminds us that God has good plans for our lives. In spite of obstacles that are always present, we must continue moving forward, trusting God to remove the obstacles and open doors.

Consider how this principle worked for Elizabeth Blackwell, America's first woman medical doctor. When she tried to open a New York City practice in 1851, no one would rent her office space because she was a woman physician. After weeks of trudging the streets, Dr. Blackwell was able to rent a room from a landlord who asked no questions.

Eventually, she attracted a few patients, almost all Quaker women who believed in equal rights for women. However, no hospital would allow Dr. Blackwell on its staff. In lieu of hospital privileges, the physician decided to create an opportunity out of that obstacle. In 1853 she opened her own small clinic in one of the city's poorest sections.

Still, people were reluctant to go to a woman physician. So Dr. Blackwell hung out a large sign announcing that all patients would be treated free of charge initially. Finally, a woman staggered into the clinic and collapsed in Blackwell's arms. Because she was in great pain, the patient didn't care who treated her.

Because of the excellent care she received from Dr. Blackwell, the patient told her friends about the "wonderful woman doctor." Soon Dr. Blackwell had a full client load and the small clinic expanded, moved, and is now a part of the New York Infirmary on East Fifteenth Street.

PRAYER

Eternal and merciful God, keep me ever aware of your constant presence in my life. Assure me and reassure me daily that you are working to bring about your good plans for me. Amen.

AFFIRMATIONS

God views me as beautiful and lovable.

God has created me talented, imaginative, and creative.

God wants the very best for me.

REFLECTION

A wise man will make more opportunities than he finds.
                                                    Francis Bacon

WEDNESDAY
Thinking Creatively

Where there is no vision, the people perish.
Proverbs 29:18
(King James Version)

Today's reading from Proverbs is a reminder that often the movement from adversity to advantage takes place when we exercise creative thinking to solve a problem.

A good lesson for all of us comes via a peasant living in eighteenth-century Russia. At that time, St. Petersburg was being developed, and the plans established would make it one of the most beautiful cities in Europe.

Before the roads and streets could be built, many large boulders brought in by a glacier from Finland had to be removed. One enormous rock was a problem. It lay in the path of one of the principal avenues in the city plans. Bids were solicited for its removal, and they were extremely high.

Of course, this is understandable, since modern excavating and removal equipment did not exist at that time. Also, there were no high-powered explosives to blast the boulder into smaller rocks. Hesitant to assume greater expense, officials pondered what to do.

Learning of the opportunity, a peasant presented himself and offered to get rid of the boulder for a much lower price than those submitted by other bidders. Since they had nothing to lose, officials gave the job to the peasant. He arrived the next morning leading a crowd of other peasants, all carrying shovels. Under his instructions, they began digging a huge hole next to the rock. The rock was propped up with timbers to prevent it from rolling into the hole. When the hole was deep enough, the timber props were removed, and the rock dropped into the hole below street level. The peasants then covered the hole and removed the excess dirt. Today ask yourself

- What "boulder" stands in the way of my progress?
- What obstacle keeps me from moving forward?
- What barrier limits my living?
- What blocks me and saps my energies?

Then, like the peasant, try to view the issue from other angles and dimensions. If you can't lift the "boulder," perhaps you can find another way to remove it.

PRAYER
Gracious and holy God, do not allow me to be blinded, bewildered, baffled, or broken by obstacles. Open my eyes and clarify my understanding so that I am resourceful, reflective, and creatively responsive. Amen.

AFFIRMATIONS
I am an open channel for God's creative energy.

God helps me create my life perfectly.

God is guiding me to the best solution.

REFLECTION
Creative minds have always been known to survive any kind of bad training.

Anna Freud

THURSDAY
God Uses Life's Bruises

Happy is the person who remains faithful under trials....
James 1:12

The writers of Scripture knew that painful experiences can serve worthy and noble purposes. They knew that, while suffering in itself is of no value, to those who wish to learn, it is a great teacher. While God does not send pain and hurt to us, *God uses life's bruises* for our good and the good of others. Here are some benefits that can emerge from our suffering:

- Increased self-confidence

- Greater faith and trust in God

- Deeper awareness of personal power and strength

- More compassion for others who suffer

- Heightened discernment of the difference between avoidable and unavoidable suffering

- More determination to eliminate the latter from our lives

- Greater capacity to love

- Less tendency to be judgmental

- More tolerance of weaknesses and shortcomings in others

- Greater patience and staying power.

Although none of us likes to suffer, the truth is that suffering can provide us with a wisdom that cannot be learned anywhere else. Suffering is the raw material God uses to make us kinder, gentler, stronger, better men and women.

PRAYER

Loving and holy God, suffering is difficult. That is why I turn to you. I give you my suffering and ask you to help me to learn from it. In that way, my sadness will turn to gladness. Amen.

AFFIRMATIONS

I surrender and I let go.

I am open to learning new truth.

I allow suffering to be my instructor.

REFLECTION

In this world, trials are not meant to take the strength out of us but to put the strength into us.

William Barclay

FRIDAY
Using the Power of Anger

Be angry, but sin not...
Psalm 4:4
(Revised Standard Version)

There is great wisdom in this biblical text. It tells us that there are times when anger is justifiable and can produce good. The issue is not our anger but how we use it. Some people let anger become a weapon to hurt others and hinder themselves. According to the Bible, the correct use of anger is to let it become a tool out of which good will result. Anger is an energy that can be utilized to move from adversity to advantage.

Actor Michael Caine is an example of someone who has used anger to move from adversity to advantage. In his autobiography, *What's It All About?* Caine tells of his deep discouragement about acting. He was living in severe poverty. His roles were small bit parts, and his sporadic income was not enough to cover his modest expenses. To survive, he also worked in a steelyard.

During that low time, he learned that his father was dying. Caine returned home and spent two days at his father's bedside before the elder Caine died. As the young actor was leaving the hospital room, a nurse ran after him. "This was in your father's pajama pocket," she said and handed him three shillings and eight pence, an amount less than ten dollars. Caine describes the energizing impact that moment held for him.

This was everything my father left to us. Nothing else, after fifty-six years of working like a beast of burden. I thanked her and walked on slowly down the long dark corridor, my heart and mind hardening with every step until they set into an unbreakable determination that I would make a success of my life and my family would never be poor again.

PRAYER

Eternal and loving God, help me use my anger creatively and to do good things with it for myself and for others. And with the passing of time, let my anger diminish to be replaced by joy and peace. Amen.

AFFIRMATIONS

God makes me strong and whole.

God gives my life meaning and purpose.

God helps me create good in my life.

REFLECTION

When I am angry, I can write, pray, and preach well, for my whole temperament is quickened, my understanding sharpened, and all mundane vexations and temptations depart.

Martin Luther

SATURDAY

Using Our Pain as a Source of Gain for Others

She is generous to the poor and needy.
Proverbs 31:20

An important aspect of moving from adversity to advantage is allowing our pain to become a source of help and healing for others. The Scripture quote for today upholds the virtue of being generous to the poor and needy.

In 1988 Linda Wiegand fell down a flight of stairs. Because of that fall, her future was changed permanently. The twenty-nine-year-old mother, who was pregnant, was on leave from her full-time job and from night school, where she was completing a master's degree in business administration. The birth turned out fine, but Wiegand's back was seriously injured. She would spend her lifetime in chronic pain. "I spent most of the day in bed," she says. "I felt useless and was consumed with self-pity."

Wanting to break her cycle of depression and despair, Wiegand asked a social worker in her community to recommend a needy family she could help. "I had to reach out to someone who was feeling a totally different kind of pain," she explains. Given a family name, Wiegand asked her husband to make some supermarket purchases that she thought a struggling family could use.

The outreach did not stop with one family. Seeing great need and deriving greater personal satisfaction, Wiegand continued helping families. Soon, others were moved by Wiegand's outreach and asked how they could help.

So began Gifts of Love, a program in which a financially able family sponsors a needy one. Hundreds of struggling families have received assistance and friendship all because Linda Wiegand let her adversity become an advantage for others.

PRAYER

Merciful God, show me how to transform my adversity for advantage to others. Through your guidance help me to use my suffering as a point of hope and help to others. Amen.

AFFIRMATIONS

My life produces positive results for myself and for others.

I am actively seeking ways to use my experiences for the good of other people.

I am using my life to make this world a better place.

REFLECTION

We are put on earth a little space,
*   That we may learn to bear*
*   the beams of love.*

William Blake

SUNDAY

Maintaining the Attitude of Gratitude

...be thankful in all circumstances.
1 Thessalonians 5:18

In the above biblical citation, Saint Paul reminds us that there is always something or someone to be thankful for. Emotionally healthy people are thankful people. They know how to count their blessings in spite of whatever hardships they have experienced. If this sounds like an impossible task, consider the late actor Bill Bixby.

Although he enjoyed starring roles in various television shows such as *My Favorite Martian, The Courtship of Eddie's Father,* and *The Incredible Hulk,* Bixby's life was not insulated from pain and sorrow. In 1981 his only child, Christopher, then six, died from a rare infection. A year later his first wife, actress Brenda Benet, committed suicide. A second marriage ended in divorce after two years. Then, Bixby was diagnosed with advanced prostate cancer that had penetrated his hipbones.

With so much trauma in one decade, Bixby might have become cynical and bitter about life. Yet he was just the opposite. "I'm the happiest that I've ever been," he said not too long before his death. "Because, as many tragedies as I've had to face in my life, I've been blessed with the greatest friends. I am privileged to work in this business."

Clearly, Bill Bixby knew how to count his blessings. While much may have gone wrong in his life, his attitude was right. In the presence of great personal trials, he found reasons to be thankful and, in so doing, celebrated life.

PRAYER

Merciful God, help me to see and appreciate the many blessings that daily flow my way: the kindness of friends, the smile of a stranger, and your constant love. Amen.

AFFIRMATIONS

I give thanks for increasing health and vitality.

I give thanks for wanting to transcend
past pains and move toward healing.

I give thanks for all of God's goodness to me.

REFLECTION

Keep your face to the sunshine, and you cannot see the shadows.

Helen Keller

MONDAY
Changing Our Language

…a fool is destroyed by his own words.
Ecclesiastes 10:12

Even the way we speak reveals whether we are cynics or celebrants of life. Our words can help or hinder our recovery. People with maturity of personality and faith have a way of speaking that is affirming and optimistic about life.

A splendid example is Mother Teresa of Calcutta. An important lesson about the right use of daily language was impressed upon Eileen Egan, one of Mother Teresa's lay workers. In *Such a Vision of the Street*, Egan tells of a day in which her conversation had been filled with a litany of problems.

After listening patiently, Mother Teresa responded, "Everything is a 'problem.' Why not use the word 'gift'?" With that simple thought, Egan says she began a major shift in her vocabulary.

Her newfound language was put to a test in the next few days when she and Mother Teresa were to fly from Vancouver to New York City. Egan was disheartened to learn the trip had to be broken en route with a long delay. She was about to inform Mother Teresa of the "problem" when she caught herself. Instead of using the word *problem*, Egan said, "Mother, I have to tell you about a gift. We have to wait four hours here, and you won't arrive at the convent until very late."

Quietly, Mother Teresa settled down in the airport to read a book of favorite meditations.

Egan says from that time on, issues that presented disappointments or difficulties would be introduced with the sentences "We have a small gift here" or "Today we have an especially big gift." Such language made everyone smile and rise to meet the challenge creatively.

PRAYER

Merciful and gracious God, help me to see the possibility in every problem, the opportunity in every obstacle, and the blessing in every burden. Amen.

AFFIRMATIONS

I affirm the beauty of the world.

I affirm that my life is moving toward wholeness.

I am relaxed, centered, and viewing the world with peace and serenity.

REFLECTION

A problem is an opportunity in work clothes.

Henry J. Raiser

TUESDAY
Living Means Giving

"…whoever wants to save his own life will lose it,
but whoever loses his life for my sake will save it."
Luke 9:24

With these words, Jesus reminds us that the movement from cynicism to celebration and from despair to hope takes place as we live our lives for others rather than for ourselves. Jesus says we are given the gift of life in order to share it, not hoard it.

We must be certain that our pain does not make us overly needy, always seeking to receive from others. Jesus tells us that the important question is not "What can I get?" but "How much can I give?" It is a spiritual law of life that in giving we receive.

Here are three suggestions for living this way:

1. Be certain that others benefit by their association with you, that they receive help and inspiration through contact with you.

2. Practice generous kindness to others, especially strangers.

3. Work to soften your judgments about people and widen your mercy. Look for good qualities, not faults, in others.

By sharing with others, we experience a double blessing. On one hand, we build stronger, healthier relationships. On the other hand, we take the focus off our own pain and see our own problems as manageable. It is in giving that we receive!

PRAYER

O Divine Master, grant that I may not seek so much
    to be consoled as to console,
    to be understood as to understand,
    to be loved as to love.

Prayer of Saint Francis of Assisi

AFFIRMATIONS

I am a lovable and loving person.

I am God's source of blessing for others.

God's light and love flow through me
and on to other people.

REFLECTION

The way to fulfill God's purpose for us, the way to true happiness, is to spend life selflessly.

William Barclay

WEDNESDAY
The Way to a Better Day

How we laughed, how we sang for joy!
Psalm 126:2

On a daily basis, the way to move from cynicism to celebration is to follow these four steps:

Think

    Thank

        Plan

            Pray

Think a better day. Upon arising from the night's rest, focus your mind on the positive. Remind yourself that this day is a gift from God, filled with wonderful possibilities.

Thank God for a better day. Before any activities begin, offer prayers of thanks and gratitude to God for the good day ahead. Remind yourself that God wants only the best for you and your life.

Plan a better day. It's amazing how many people simply drift from one day to the next. Consequently, they have no organizing vision for living. Begin each day with a short list of objectives. This will give you a sense of direction.

Pray a better day. It is a good spiritual discipline to begin and end each day with prayer and meditation. Pray for guidance to make the day better for others. At the end of the day, thank God for the blessings you encountered.

PRAYER

Loving and kind God, guide me to make life better for others and for myself every day. Help me organize my time and my talents to bring you glory. Amen.

AFFIRMATIONS

Today I will make a list of goals and objectives.

Today I will make plans for my life.

Today I will diligently follow my daily goals, objectives, and plans.

REFLECTION

The longest journey
Is the journey inwards
Of him who has chosen his destiny,
Who has started upon his quest.

Dag Hammarskjöld

THURSDAY
The Faith-and-Happiness Link

"Your joy will be complete."
John 16:24
(*New International Version*)

Jesus is concerned about our happiness and joy. In the gospels, he links faith and happiness many times, clearly implying that those who trust and believe in God will be people of joy. Interestingly, a recent Gallup poll revealed that people of faith are twice as likely as those with weaker spiritual commitments to describe themselves as "very happy."

The leading "happiness researcher" in the United States is David Myers, Ph.D., professor of psychology at Hope College in Holland, Michigan. Along with faith, Dr. Myers cites the following attributes and activities which encourage and promote happiness:

- A fit and healthy body

- Realistic goals and expectations

- Positive self-esteem

- Feelings of control

- Optimism

- An outgoing attitude toward others

- Supportive friendships that enable companionship and confiding

- A socially intimate, sexually warm, quitable marriage

- Challenging work and active leisure punctuated by rest and retreat

- A faith that entails communal support, purpose, acceptance, outward focus, and hope.

As you read this list, consider what part of your life is deficient. Then begin making plans to correct that area of your life so you can begin experiencing the full joy of which Jesus speaks.

PRAYER

Eternal and gracious God, continue moving my life in the direction of joy. Help me to be a happy disciple. Amen.

AFFIRMATIONS

I have the right to peace and happiness.

I love and accept myself completely.

I deserve the best and the best is flowing to me now.

REFLECTION

Laugh and grow strong.

Ignatius of Loyola

FRIDAY
Turning Life's Stresses Over to God

He strengthens those who are weak and tired.
Isaiah 40:29

The late Norman Vincent Peale, author of *The Power of Positive Thinking*, tells of a stressful time when he was on the verge of a nervous breakdown. As a young minister, he was called to serve a large church in a university community, one normally served by a more experienced pastor. Many of the people in his congregation were professors at the university as well as leaders of the city.

Wanting to justify the confidence of those who gave him such an outstanding opportunity, the young Rev. Peale worked very hard to make each of his sermons extremely intellectual and filled with penetrating insights and to deliver them with great eloquence. Soon this pressure became unbearable. He was constantly tired, nervous, and without energy.

Sensing he was about to collapse emotionally, Dr. Peale wisely sought help from a professor who had become a good friend. The young pastor confided in the academic that he had used up all his emotional reserve and felt he was about to have a nervous breakdown. After listening, the professor made an unusual suggestion. He asked Dr. Peale to lie on the sofa, close his eyes, and listen while the professor read a passage to him. Dr. Peale was surprised when the man read from Isaiah (40:28-31): "He strengthens those who are weak and tired....those who trust in the LORD for help will find their strength renewed."

That passage, the professor told Dr. Peale, from Isaiah is a power formula. It urges us to depend upon God for support and energy. More than four decades later Dr. Peale recalled: "I continue to follow my friend's advice and it has never failed me. My life is crowded with activity but that formula gives me all the strength I need."

PRAYER

Gracious Lord, help me tap into your power, strength, and energy. Help me let go and trust you to meet my daily needs. Amen.

AFFIRMATIONS

As I turn to God, things come to me easily and effortlessly.

As I turn to God, perfect wisdom comes from my heart.

As I turn to God, my life blossoms and blooms.

REFLECTION

There is no problem, difficulty, or defeat that you cannot solve or overcome by faith, positive thinking, and prayer to God.

Norman Vincent Peale

SATURDAY
Making the Commitment Not to Suffer

So then, let us rid ourselves of everything
that gets in the way...
and let us run with determination
the race that lies before us.
Hebrews 12:1

The journey from cynicism to celebration is smoother and quicker when we make a commitment not to suffer. We must take a stand for ourselves and for our lives by choosing not to suffer. Such a commitment is a profound statement of self-respect. It creates vitality, energy, and joy in place of inertia, resignation, and torment.

Jane, a thirty-year-old mother of four, was sexually abused as a child by various members of her extended family. Today Jane lives hundreds of miles away from her family of origin. Yet whenever her father telephones, Jane is left feeling extremely depressed for days afterward as a result of his continuing verbal and emotional abuse during the conversations.

Finally, she made the commitment not to suffer any longer and wrote him not to telephone her again. "It was hard to do, but I feel so much better not hearing from him," she says. "The best thing I ever did for myself was to write him and say that I found his conversations with me insensitive, demeaning, and abusive and that I did not want him to telephone me again. I also told him if my feelings changed, I would let him know."

PRAYER

Loving God, as I make the commitment not to suffer, I ask you to strengthen my resolve, deepen my will power, and guide me day by day. Amen.

AFFIRMATIONS

I am willing to be happy.

I am willing to pay the price.

I am willing to end my suffering.

REFLECTION

Don't wait for other people to be happy for you. Any happiness you get, you've got to make yourself.

Alice Walker

SUNDAY
The Power of Friendship

Two are better off than one....
If one of them falls down,
the other can help him up.
Ecclesiastes 4:9-10

Even though our family of origin may have hurt or abandoned us, we must not minimize the value of friendship. Friends become our family of *choice.* Such friendships can provide us with tremendous support.

A good friend can

- allow us to express our fears, sorrows, and dreams
- lift us above self-criticism
- clarify our distorted self-image
- reveal our breadth and possibilities
- highlight the positive
- modify the negative
- celebrate our victories
- sympathize with our defeats.

A friend can provide the ray of sunshine we all need to remove the dark clouds hanging over our lives. There is great wisdom in the biblical statement "Two are better off than one."

PRAYER

Loving God, I come in contact with many people each day. Lead me to develop good friendships. Help me to feel safe in opening up and confiding in another person. Amen.

AFFIRMATIONS

I have the courage to confide in another person.

I am strong enough to become vulnerable.

Today I will give love and appreciation to others.

REFLECTION

A friend may well be reckoned the masterpiece of Nature.
Ralph Waldo Emerson

MONDAY
Practicing Patience

There is an appointed time for everything…
A time to weep, and a time to laugh.
Ecclesiastes 3:1, 4
(*New American Bible*)

An ancient Persian legend tells of a king who wanted to discourage his four sons from making hasty, rash judgments. He sent his oldest son on a winter journey to see a mango tree. When spring came, the next son was sent on the same journey. Summer followed, and the third son was sent. Finally, after the youngest son made the visit in the autumn, the king called them together and asked them to describe the mango tree.

The first son said it looked like a large burnt stump. The second son disagreed and described the mango tree as lovely, large, and green. The third son said the other two were misinformed; the tree was filled with blossoms as beautiful as the rose. The fourth declared that all of his brothers were wrong; the mango was full of luscious fruit.

Of course, the young men were confused by these conflicting descriptions of the same tree. So the king said, "Each of you is right." He went on to explain that each of his sons saw the mango tree in a different season. Thus, each one correctly described what he saw. "However," the king continued, "the lesson for you is to withhold your judgment until you have seen the tree in all its seasons."

This same instruction is applicable to those whose inner child has been bruised. As a hurting person, you should practice patience. "There is a time to weep, and a time to laugh." In the weeping time, withhold judgment until the "season" of hurting has gone through its cycle of acute pain, anxiety, accommodation, adjustment, acceptance, and—eventually—joy and laughter.

Don't decide today that your pain is too great, that your suffering will never end, that you cannot bear the hurt any longer. Exercise patience!

PRAYER

Loving God, teach me the art of patience. Help me to cultivate this biblical virtue in my life. Empower me to work and wait for good results. Amen.

AFFIRMATIONS

Divine love fills me now.

Divine light brightens my life.

Divine love is preparing me for health, happiness, and wholeness.

REFLECTION

Only with winter patience can we bring the deep-desired, long-awaited spring.

Anne Morrow Lindbergh

TUESDAY
Recognizing Growth and Recovery

Jesus grew both in body and in wisdom,
gaining favor with God and men.
Luke 2:52

One of the sad facts of life is that there are people who grow older without growing into maturity and wholeness. Of course, individuals who are fundamentally healthy always seek physical, emotional, and spiritual growth. Here is a short list to help you recognize when growth and recovery are taking place:

- Concern for others outweighs concern for ourselves.

- Balance replaces extremes.

- Seasoned confidence replaces uneasy feelings of insecurity and self-doubt.

- Healthy choices are more numerous than unhealthy ones.

- The presence of a hurtful person is detected before the hurt is inflicted.

- Emotions are respected but tempered with reason and responsibility.

- There is courage of conviction.

- The awareness of others' needs is matched by compassion and involvement.

- There is a profound willingness to change.

- There is understanding of a task and patience to see it through.

- There is wisdom as well as knowledge.

Of course, we never arrive but always seek movement toward objectives of physical, emotional, and spiritual growth.

PRAYER

Loving God, day by day let the child Jesus be a model for me. Like him, let me grow in wisdom, in spirit, and in every part of my inner life. Amen.

AFFIRMATIONS

I am accepting life's challenges.

I am accomplishing my goals with more and more ease.

I am willing to expand and grow.

REFLECTION

Grown up. That is a terribly hard thing to do. It is much easier to skip it and go from one childhood to another.

F. Scott Fitzgerald

WEDNESDAY
Eliminating Growth Barriers

*"I have come in order that you might have life—
life in all its fullness."*
John 10:10

In this biblical text, Jesus declares that a key aspect of his ministry was to help us experience lives filled with joy and meaning. However, often growth into the full life can be sabotaged by our attitudes. Here are seven barriers to growth to be on guard against:

1. Constantly nursing grudges and resentment.

2. Reliving the past; never enjoying the present; and not looking toward a brighter, better future.

3. Fighting events and people that cannot possibly be changed.

4. Feeling sorry for yourself and engaging in self-pity.

5. Retreat and withdrawal from the world and the company of fine, decent people.

6. Not accepting and appreciating yourself and your many talents,m contributions, and positive personality aspects.

7. Expecting immediate results and then suffering major depression because you have not allowed enough time for movement from grieving to growing.

If you discover a combination of these working against you, the best way to balance them is to reorient your thinking. Try to reframe your thoughts into more optimistic views by believing the best, hoping for the best, and praying for God's best in your life.

PRAYER

Merciful and loving God, thank you for sending Jesus the Christ to lead me into full, vibrant living. Keep my thoughts oriented to this spiritual truth, and move me day by day toward this reality. Amen.

AFFIRMATIONS

I am loving God with my whole heart.

I am loving my neighbor as myself.

I am loving and enjoying life.

REFLECTION

The mind is its own place, and in it self
Can make a Heaven of Hell, a Hell of heaven.

John Milton

THURSDAY
Managing Crises Creatively

For the Spirit that God has given us does not make us timid;
instead, his Spirit fills us with power, love, and self-control.
2 Timothy 1:7

The awareness of earlier abuse always results in emotional turmoil. Thus, it becomes crucial to find ways of creatively managing such a personal crisis. Here are five steps for crisis management:

1. *View events optimistically.* Various studies show that optimists are happier, healthier, and better problem solvers. Pessimists, on the other hand, tend to cope poorly with crises. An optimist views life saying, "At least now I know what is wrong and can begin doing the necessary repair work."

2. *Take one step at a time.* Some traumas are so great that it may be difficult if not impossible to view them optimistically. In such cases, it is important simply to think about the next step. Try breaking things down into small segments. Rather than asking, "How can I cope with my life?" try asking, "How can I get through the next hour or the remainder of the day?"

3. *Do an evaluation.* While optimism is crucial, it is important not to be naive. Look carefully at your life and the damage that was inflicted. Without soft pedaling the facts, evaluate where you are, what needs to

be done, and how to do it. One woman who could no longer bear the pain of earlier abuse decided she needed to be in therapy. Because her insurance did not cover the fees, she took an additional part-time job to cover the extra expense.

4. *Take concrete action.* Develop an action plan for recovery. This can include taking care of your body physically through an exercise regimen, taking care of your emotional life by joining a support group, or nurturing your mind through a reading program.

5. *Exercise your faith.* During times of personal upheaval, many have found that their faith is vital to coping with a personal crisis. Don't hesitate to seek out direction from a trusted spiritual leader. If you have not been in the habit of attending worship services regularly, this would be a very good time to begin.

PRAYER

Loving and merciful God, as I deal with the pain of my past, I ask you to give me your spirit of power, love, and self-control. Amen.

AFFIRMATIONS

I am moving forward one step at a time.

I am responding creatively to each event.

I am trusting God to guide me.

REFLECTION

Who except God can give you peace? Has the world ever been able to satisfy the heart?

Saint Gerard Majella

FRIDAY
Life After Pain

*Your life will be brighter than
sunshine at noon.*
Job 11:17

This biblical text became a reality for Job, who suffered greatly. We must always remember that we are not the only ones who suffer. History is filled with women and men who suffered *and* overcame their suffering. There *is* life after pain. Allow yourself to be inspired by the following individuals, who turned burdens into blessings:

- *Abraham Lincoln,* raised in abject poverty and suffering, grew from severe depression to become a great president.

- *Helen Keller,* deaf and blind from early infancy, became a world-renowned author, lecturer, and advocate for the deaf and blind.

- *O. J. Simpson,* raised in a ghetto and afflicted with such severe rickets due to malnutrition that his legs were permanently deformed, grew into a celebrated professional athlete.

- *Itzhak Perlman,* paralyzed from the waist down at age four, grew into an incomparable concert violinist.

PRAYER

Loving God, help me to recall those courageous women and men who have overcome their pain. Help me turn pain into power, trial into triumph, and grieving into growing. Amen.

AFFIRMATIONS

I am turning suffering into triumph.

I am turning burdens into blessings.

I am accepting life in spite of my pain.

REFLECTION

There must be acceptance and the knowledge that sorrow fully accepted brings its own gifts. For there is an alchemy in sorrow. It can be transmuted into wisdom, which, if it does not bring joy, can yet bring happiness.

Pearl S. Buck

SATURDAY
Tapping Our Interior Potential

I am Wisdom, and I have insight;
I have knowledge and sound judgment.
Proverbs 8:12

Geologists tell us that only three percent of the earth's fresh water is on the surface of the planet in the form of rivers and lakes. The other ninety-seven percent remains hidden as a huge subterranean reservoir.

During the last century in Artois, France, a hole was dug two thousand feet into the ground, and from it a fountain of water rose two hundred ninety feet into the air. It began to gush forth at the rate of one million gallons of water per day. The term *artesian* is derived from the name of the French village Artois.

Human potential is much the same: three percent on the surface and ninety-seven percent below. Those who recover from inner-child abuse are those who have been able to tap into their hidden potential, talents, energies, and strengths. As the crisis emerges and the pain deepens, they dig deep below the surface and tap the infinite reservoir within. This allows concealed powers of human personality to overflow onto the surface.

It is then that these survivors discover the "insight, knowledge, and sound judgment" cited into today's biblical text. Because they draw upon the ninety-seven percent below, they are able to manage their crisis creatively and give birth to new experiences, increased opportunities, and greater growth.

PRAYER

Loving God, I thank you for creating me with great potential. Help me respond with faith and creativity to the painful issues of my life. Amen.

AFFIRMATIONS

I am tapping into my wisdom and insight.

I am naturally enlightened.

I have everything I need to enjoy living.

REFLECTION

Most people live...in a very restricted circle of their potential being....Great emergencies and crises show us how much greater our vital resources are than we had supposed.

William James

SUNDAY

Becoming Stronger in Broken Places

They grow stronger as they go.
Psalm 84:7

This six-word sentence from Psalm 84 expresses the powerful truth that overcoming one trauma empowers us to overcome a second one. When we triumph over one pain, we find it easier to master the next one. In *The New Revised Standard Version* of the Bible, this text reads, "They go from strength to strength." The pattern of moving from strength to strength is a common characteristic of all survivors.

Psychologist Ann Kaiser Stearns interviewed dozens of people whose tragedies, disappointments, and losses were turned into victories. In her book *Coming Back: Rebuilding Lives After Crisis and Loss*, she offers the following hopeful observation:

> Some triumphant survivors are extraordinary individuals and have unusual strengths; most aren't. Most of the people I studied were regular human beings with the usual frailties and vulnerabilities. Those who have made comebacks, however, do show certain ways of thinking which set them apart.

Dr. Stearns goes on to cite several attitudes that she says are crucial for moving "from strength to strength."

- I will not be defeated.
- I will vividly examine the future.
- I will take advantage of available opportunities.
- I will not assume the victim posture.
- I can do it if I set my mind.
- I have to be willing to expand.
- I will accept life's challenge.
- I will find a way to get what I want.

PRAYER

Most merciful God, I offer you praise because you are guiding me in the movement from hurting to healing. Continue to help me heal every day and in every way. Amen.

AFFIRMATIONS

I refuse to remain in pain.
I accept the flow of God's healing.
I am open to receiving all of God's blessings upon my life today.

REFLECTION

The world breaks everyone and afterward many are strong at the broken places.

Ernest Hemingway

MONDAY
Life Is Biased on the Side of Healing

"I will...bandage those that are hurt,
and heal those that are sick."
Ezekiel 34:16

We are created to heal and recover from wounds. This can be seen in the most basic of injuries. When we accidentally cut ourselves, scar tissue forms, and before long, the skin is as good as new. The same principle applies to life's larger damages.

The truth of this observation can be seen vividly in the life of Linda Wachner, at the time of this writing the only female CEO of a Fortune 500 industrial company. However, there was a time when those who knew her could never have imagined Wachner would enjoy such success. She was born with back problems. By the time she was eleven, physicians concluded that surgery was necessary to correct increasingly severe scoliosis.

Linda's parents were told the risks were great. Without surgery, their little girl would live in great pain, and her physical deformity would increase. While the surgery could relieve pain and correct the curvature of her spine, there was a high possibility that it would leave their daughter paralyzed.

After much discussion, the family opted for surgery. For a year, the eleven-year-old lay flat on her back, encased in a plaster cast from her head to her knees. It was a time of great uncertainty.

When the cast was to be removed, it was not clear whether

or not Linda Wachner would be able to walk. At best, she would have to relearn walking. During that year when she felt so helpless and vulnerable, the little girl resolved that she would overcome her condition, no matter what the outcome.

Today she credits her success to lessons learned while flat on her back. "The focus I have today comes from that time in my life," she says. "When you want to walk again, you learn how to focus on that with all your might, and you don't stop until you do it."

For those hurting from pains inflicted upon the inner child, Linda Wachner is a powerful reminder that life's bias is in favor of healing and results in our recovery from any wound.

PRAYER

Merciful God, thank you for the realization that what was broken can be repaired, that what was hurt can be healed, that what was damaged can be restored. Amen.

AFFIRMATIONS

Today health and energy flow to me.

Today beauty and joy fill me.

Today I am being filled with spiritual power.

REFLECTION

The whole Universe is on your side. Life is forever biased on the side of healing, on the side of overcoming, on the side of success. Whenever you get yourself centered in the Universal flow, you become synchronized with this divine bias for good.

Eric Butterworth

TUESDAY
Experiencing Happiness

"I have told you this so that…your joy may be complete."
John 15:11

Those who have suffered abuse often exhibit patterns of severe negative thinking. They often view life as a half-empty glass rather than as one that is half full. They also have a strong tendency to focus only upon what is wrong in their lives. Such thought patterns prevent the spirit from experiencing the joy and happiness that Jesus speaks of in today's Scripture.

Yet psychologists know that happiness can be experienced when negative thinking is reduced and even eliminated. This can be done by following these five simple steps:

1. *Consciously interrupt your negative thoughts.* When you find yourself dwelling on the negatives, immediately interrupt your thinking. Go for a walk, call a friend long distance, write a letter to encourage someone, watch a favorite video.

2. *Surround yourself with optimistic people.* Cultivate the friendship of people who see the world through rose-colored glasses. Avoid those who are harsh pessimists.

3. *Write out a list of positive aspects in your life.* No one lives a life totally filled with negatives. Take a good look and write out what is pleasant and positive in your life. You will be amazed at how much the good outweighs the bad. Review the list frequently and add to it.

4. *Don't globalize set-backs.* Just because you have a difficult, depressing day does not mean that every day of your
   life will be the same. Weather the storm, but enjoy the
   days of bright sunshine.

5. *Stop criticizing yourself.* You may be your own worst enemy by constantly reminding yourself of every failure and
   shortcoming. Today begin practicing self-acceptance. If
   there are aspects of your life you do not like, take a positive step. Resolve to make changes rather than simply
   criticizing yourself.

PRAYER

*Gracious God, sometimes my eyes are blinded and my ears
are deafened to the many blessings of my life. Help me to
see and to hear the beauty in me and around me. Amen.*

AFFIRMATIONS

My life is rich and abundant.

God sends good gifts my way.

My outlook deepens with optimism every day.

REFLECTION

*God, give us grace to accept with serenity
   the things that cannot be changed,
   courage to change the things which should be changed,
   and the wisdom to distinguish the one from the other.*
                                        Reinhold Niebuhr

WEDNESDAY
Awareness of Healing

The Lord...heals the broken-hearted
and bandages their wounds.
Psalm 147:2-3

Again, Scripture assures us that God seeks to heal us from every human hurt. Often our healing is so gradual that we may not even be aware of it at first. However, we can be assured that healing is taking place when we notice some of the following changes in our lives:

- We feel comfortable doing things ourselves.

- We want to have an intimate relationship.

- We are able to verbalize feelings as they emerge.

- We are more gentle with ourselves.

- We can reach out to other people.

- We are more honest with ourselves and with other people.

- We can direct anger accurately and appropriately.

- We are no longer struggling just to cope day by day.

- We feel more nourished, balanced, and whole.

As you review this list, commend yourself for parts of it that apply to you now. Remind yourself to be patient where you fall short. Healing takes time, but it does take place!

PRAYER

Loving God, teach me not to fear the darkness but to love the light more. In every way, day by day, do your work of healing in my life. Amen.

AFFIRMATIONS

Day by day, I feel happier for being alive.

Day by day, I feel more vibrant and healthy.

Day by day, I feel more relaxed and centered.

REFLECTION

The wish for healing has ever been the half of health.

Seneca

THURSDAY
Asking God to Heal Our Wounds

The LORD is near to those who are discouraged;
he saves those who have lost all hope.
Psalm 34:18

Along with our own efforts to achieve healing and wholeness, we must not hesitate to ask God for his healing. We must always remember that this is a God who notices and responds to human hurt. Neil Mintzman was not a religious person, but he prayed for an answer to why his twenty-year-old daughter, Stacey, had been taken from him ten years earlier in a freak auto accident. Time had done little to heal his wound. He simply could not come to terms with the reality of his loss.

Then one night while he was asleep, a "Presence of magnificent light suddenly filled my dream," as he puts it. "Though I did not see its face, I knew it was God. I asked, 'Stacey? How is Stacey?' and the Presence replied, 'She is happy; she is loved.' Through tears, I repeated my question and received the same answer."

Sensing the dream was about to end, Mintzman spoke again to the Presence: "But I must have a sign. Something tangible to ease my pain." The Presence replied: "Open your eyes!" However, Mintzman was hesitant to do it without first receiving a sign. This time the Presence commanded the grieving father to open his eyes, and he did.

The first thing Mintzman saw were the red numerals on the digital clock glowing in the dark by his bed. He stared at them in disbelief. The numbers read 5:22. "That was the month and day my darling Stacey died," he says. "I had my sign." From that moment on, his pain was relieved.

PRAYER

Loving God, let your healing graces flow through me and make me whole. Let my entire life become a great witness to your unfailing presence. Amen.

AFFIRMATIONS

I give thanks for divine restoration.

I give thanks for the healing love of
God flowing through me.

I affirm God's desire for my healing and wholeness.

REFLECTION

Having poured out our heart to God, we need to listen, to keep our heart open both for his response and his action within us.

George Appleton

FRIDAY
Understanding Guilt

"O God, I am too ashamed to raise my head in your presence."
Ezra 9:6

Today's verse serves as a reminder that everyone suffers from feelings of guilt, including those who wrote sacred Scripture. An important step in making the transition from cynicism to celebration is understanding and responding to guilt feelings. When handled properly, guilt is an emotion that leads to liberation. On the other hand, guilt can cause great damage when poorly managed. There is healthy guilt and unhealthy guilt.

Healthy guilt is to the conscience what soul is to the body: a signal that something is wrong. For example, if I have over-reacted to a situation and said cruel, unkind words, it is appropriate for me to feel guilty. This guilt can motivate me to undo the harm I have done, apologize, and resolve not to repeat such actions. This kind of guilt produces positive results.

However, intertwined with healthy guilt can be neurotic or unhealthy guilt. An example might be a man who feels guilty about plans to marry a woman because his mother does not approve of her. The man struggles with two choices. He can terminate the relationship and reduce his guilt concerning the mother. On the other hand, he can go ahead with the marriage and feel continuing, unresolved guilt. This kind of guilt is inappropriate and only hinders our growth.

The following questions can help you determine whether you suffer from healthy or unhealthy guilt:

- Am I feeling guilt because of pressure other people are putting on me?

- Am I feeling guilty because of perfectionism and setting unreasonable goals for myself?

- Am I feeling guilt because I have a need to please everyone?

If you answered yes to these questions, you may rightly suspect that your guilt is unhealthy. To be certain, however, find a good friend or religious leader to confide in. Ask that person to help you sort through guilt feelings.

PRAYER

Merciful and kind God, give me spiritual discernment to know the difference between healthy and unhealthy guilt. When I am wrong, help me to do what is right and good. Amen.

AFFIRMATIONS

God loves me, so I love and accept myself.

Because I love myself, I do not have to please everyone.

God wants the best for me, and I am open to all God's blessings for me.

REFLECTION

We must not be afraid or embarrassed to talk about our feelings of guilt with those who have been trained to help us when the going gets rough.

Granger Westberg

SATURDAY
Responding to Guilt

*"And so I do my best always to have a clear
conscience before God and man."*
Acts of the Apostles 24:16

Because we all experience guilt at times, it is important to handle it in a constructive way. Here is a five-step process for responding to guilt.

1. *Acknowledge the guilt feelings.* If you are feeling uneasy and guilty over some words or behavior, admit it freely and openly to yourself.

2. Ask yourself *whether the guilt is healthy or unhealthy.* As stated in yesterday's meditation, not all guilt is appropriate. Examine yours to determine whether it is appropriate or inappropriate guilt. Examine your conscience carefully to be certain your guilt feelings do not stem from unrealistic or unhealthy expectations.

3. *Make amends for true guilt.* Admit your fault to the person who has been offended. Apologize sincerely. Ask for forgiveness. Do this without too much self-blame. Remind yourself that you are human and that you are now doing your best to make amends.

4. *Learn from the situation.* After making amends, re-examine the situation and try to learn from it so it is less likely to happen again. Remind yourself that this event

can be turned into an enriching experience that leaves you stronger that you were before.

5. *Give guilt feelings time to recede.* Usually, the mere fact of acknowledging and making amends does not make guilt feelings disappear immediately. Strong emotions take time to recede. Often it is healthier to think in terms of *reducing* guilt rather than erasing it.

PRAYER

Most holy and compassionate God, when I wrong someone else, let me be quick to make amends, seek forgiveness, and move on. Amen.

AFFIRMATIONS

I have the insight to recognize my wrongs.

I have the maturity to make amends.

I take responsibility for my actions.

REFLECTION

To regret deeply is to live afresh.

Henry David Thoreau

SUNDAY
Transforming Pain Into Compassion

"...we must help the weak, remembering the words
that the Lord Jesus himself said,
'There is more happiness in giving than in receiving.'"
Acts of the Apostles 20:35

Healthy people know how to transform their misfortune into compassion for others. It is a sign of emotional and spiritual maturity to touch another person with kindness. Healthy men and women do not allow themselves to become calloused and hardened, withdrawing from people. Rather, they use their pain as an incentive to help others heal.

Consider Eleanor Roosevelt, who was born into the type of family that today would be labeled "dysfunctional." When Eleanor was only four, her emotionally remote mother declared to her, "You have no looks." Such a cruel comment from a parent could have destroyed the young girl's self-esteem. Four years later, Eleanor's mother died.

Eleanor's father, the youngest brother of President Theodore Roosevelt, was an alcoholic. Like many alcoholics, his behavior was inconsistent and irresponsible. He died when Eleanor was ten. Now little Eleanor Roosevelt was an orphan.

Any child raised under such severe conditions might easily have grown up to be cold, hard, detached, and withholding. Yet Eleanor matured into an unusually warm, generous, kind, and compassionate woman. She continues to be cited as one of the most admired Americans. One person who met Eleanor

Roosevelt and experienced her warmth was Blanche Wiesen Cook, Ph.D. Dr. Cook, professor of history and women's studies at City University of New York, says Eleanor Roosevelt understood the pain of others because of her own painful life. Dr. Cook writes of her encounter with Eleanor Roosevelt,

> I was lucky enough to meet her in the late 1950s, and when we were introduced, she smiled, took my hand, and looked me straight in the eye. She did the same with everyone she met because she truly loved all people. Wherever she went and whenever she spoke, people knew instantly that her view of the world included them.

PRAYER

Merciful God, teach me how to transform my pain into compassion for others. Let my suffering become the source of goodness, kindness, and even redemption for others. Amen.

AFFIRMATIONS

God is using me to help others today.

God's light and love flow through me.

As God heals me, I will help heal others.

REFLECTION

I believe happiness is bound up with helpfulness. I believe our job is to reach out for bigger things rather than to curl up in our own little shells and snarl at the world.

Jerry Fleishman

MONDAY
Making a Difference for Someone

...be kind and tender-hearted to one another....
Ephesians 4:32

Our own pain should never prevent us from reaching out and helping another person. Consider the case of Ellen C. By age thirty, she had been through two drug and alcohol rehabilitation centers but had never managed to remain sober for longer than ten months at a time. She had battled the ravages of alcoholism since age fourteen.

Ellen could not identify any accomplishments of which she could be proud. She was convinced she would never marry nor have children. She felt her life had been a mistake and a waste. In despair, she seriously considered suicide.

However, God brought to her mind a man she had met at an Alcoholics Anonymous meeting. She called and spoke with him. During the conversation, her deep-seated frustration and anger emerged. She was angry at her parents, her family, her Alcoholics Anonymous group, even God. "How could God do this to me?" she shouted at the man on the other end of the phone.

Her friend did not become angry. He was kind and compassionate, listening carefully. He allowed Ellen to unload years of stored-up anger. As the friendship grew, he helped Ellen get into a detoxification center. During her hospitalization, the man called, visited, and continued to encourage her. He repeatedly reminded her that she was a special and beautiful person, created and loved by God and placed on earth for a unique purpose. He never gave up on her.

Two years later, Ellen has remained sober. She has found God and gained both peace and serenity in her life. She was overwhelmed to learn that the man she called in desperation had just lost his son. The young man was killed in an alcohol-related accident.

No matter how great our own pain, we can still make a difference for someone!

PRAYER

Lord Jesus, teach me to be generous;
To give and not count the cost;
To fight and not heed the wounds;
To toil and not seek for rest;
To labor and not seek any reward
Except that of knowing that I do your will. Amen.

(Adapted from a prayer
of Saint Ignatius of Loyola)

AFFIRMATIONS

I will let my pain become gain for others.

I will use my pain as a creative energy to
bring people help and hope.

Today I will be a healer in spite of my own wounds.

REFLECTION

Knowing sorrow well, I learn the way to succor the distressed.

Virgil

TUESDAY

The Importance of Spontaneous Kindness

*Remember those who are suffering, as though
you were suffering as they are.*
Hebrews 13:3

Dwight Morrow, father of Anne Morrow Lindbergh, hosted a dinner party at which Calvin Coolidge was present. After Coolidge left, Morrow told the remaining guests that Coolidge would make a good president. The others disagreed. They felt Coolidge was too quiet; that he lacked color, personality, and presence; and that no one would like him.

Then six-year-old Anne spoke up: "I like him!" When asked why, the little girl displayed a small bandaged finger. "He was the only one at the party who asked about my sore finger," she explained. "And that's why he would make a good president."

That incident is an invaluable life lesson for moving from callousness to compassion. Like Calvin Coolidge, a presidential candidate, we must not become too busy, too important, too preoccupied with our own affairs and neglect the needs of others.

PRAYER

*Loving God, open my eyes to the pain of others. Help me
see a hurt and heal it, help me see a need and fill it, help me
see anxiety and ease it.*

AFFIRMATIONS

Today I will reach out to anyone who needs me.

Today I will use my experiences to help others.

Today I make myself available as an
agent of God's healing love.

REFLECTION

Always set a high value on spontaneous kindness.

Samuel Johnson

WEDNESDAY
Experience Healing Through Helping

"Share your food with the hungry and
open your homes to the homeless poor....
and your wounds will be quickly healed."
Isaiah 58:7-8

It is a law of life that we can experience healing through helping. By actively sharing with others and opening our lives to them, our own wounds are diminished, reduced, and even eliminated. Too often, however, our own hurts seem so great that we are blinded to the needs of others. Important to the process of recovery is taking time to consider what kind of person you have become as a result of abuse. Are you like a reservoir, a canal, or a swamp?

A reservoir is a place where water is stored so it is available when needed. Are you a reservoir person? Are you an individual whom others can call upon when they are down? Are you a trustee of God's blessings and gifts, able to share them with those who are less fortunate?

Or are you like a canal? The function of a canal is to channel water from one place to another in an orderly fashion. A canal holds water only temporarily. Are you a canal person? Are you an individual who makes a connecting link between people? Are you a person who can connect hurting people to sources of help and hope?

Or have you become a swamp? A swamp differs from both

a reservoir and a canal in that it has an inlet but no outlet; water flows in but not out. The result is stagnation. The water spoils and the many living things in it begin to die out. Has your abuse made you a swamp? Are you a completely needy, dependent person always grasping for more and more from others but never giving?

Today's Scripture reminds us that we can experience healing by helping. It reminds us that recovery is greatly facilitated as we "share our food with the hungry" and "open our homes to the homeless poor."

PRAYER

Eternal and loving God, in spite of my past pains, help me to be more like a reservoir and a canal and less like a swamp. Empower me to reach out to others out with understanding, compassion, sensitivity. Amen.

AFFIRMATIONS

I accept and love the challenge of reaching out to others.

I freely and lovingly provide support wherever it is needed.

I am a responsible, powerful, and loving person.

REFLECTION

What do we live for if it is not to make life less difficult for each other.

George Eliot

THURSDAY
The Importance of Thoughtful Acts

"…your light must shine before people, so that they will see the good things you do and praise your Father in heaven."
Matthew 5:16

Those who have experienced the transition from hurting to healing and from pain to peace will want to offer thanks to God by treating others with thoughtfulness and kindness. Thoughtfulness comes in many forms. Kind acts are always welcomed by recipients. Life provides us with ample opportunities to be thoughtful.

- A thoughtful person is quick to send a note of encouragement to someone who is feeling low.

- A thoughtful person will offer a compliment to someone who has received a promotion, an honor, or other accomplishment.

- A thoughtful person offers to run errands, pick up groceries, mail letters, and so on, for someone who is housebound.

- A thoughtful person visits family and friends who are hospitalized.

- A thoughtful person parks a bit farther from a store, allowing the elderly or parents with several small children to have the closer spaces.

- A thoughtful person responds promptly when hearing about a nearby crisis, offering to help in practical ways.

According to Jesus, thoughtful people are a gift to the world. They don't wait for opportunities; they create them. In the process, they make the world a better place. They make others happy, including themselves.

PRAYER

Eternal and merciful God, I thank you for my progress and recovery. Now I offer my life to become a source of blessing to others for your glory. Amen.

AFFIRMATIONS

Today I will act thoughtfully toward everyone I encounter.

Today I will express my gratitude to God through kind acts.

Today I will be a source of hope and help for someone else.

REFLECTION

So many gods, so many creeds,
So many paths that wind and wind,
While just the art of being kind
Is all this sad world needs.

Ella Wheeler Wilcox

FRIDAY
The Power of a Kind Act

So then, you must clothe yourselves with compassion,
kindness, humility, gentleness, and patience.
Colossians 3:12

To celebrate the bicentennial of the Constitution, former First Lady Barbara Bush appeared on an ABC-TV special filmed before a live audience of eight hundred thousand. Earlier in the day, Mrs. Bush had met a sixty-two-year-old retired construction worker who was to read the Constitution's Preamble. He had only recently learned to read and was so nervous about appearing on television that he wanted to cancel just hours before the program was to air.

With great patience and first-class kindness, Mrs. Bush drew his fears out. When he explained there were words he didn't understand, Mrs. Bush said she ran into words like that as well. Then she suggested they read the Preamble together. On stage, the duo began to read. As the man's confidence grew, Barbara Bush lowered her voice until it was eventually just a whisper.

The ability to treat others with consummate kindness is a sign of maturity and integrity. It is a strong indicator that one is at peace with the world.

PRAYER

Eternal and merciful God, open the eyes of my heart to the multitude of opportunities all around me for practicing kindness. Amen.

AFFIRMATIONS

Today I will make a difference for someone.

Today I will pay an unexpected compliment.

Today I will be a source of joy to another person.

REFLECTION

Kindness in words creates confidence.
Kindness in thinking creates profoundness.
Kindness in giving creates love.

Lao Tze

SATURDAY
Making Room for Others

"I was a stranger and you received me in your homes...."
Matthew 25:35

Because our own wounds sometimes feel so great, it is easy to forget or neglect the needs of others. Therefore, we must always be on the lookout for opportunities to exercise compassion and thereby keep it alive in our heart. The word *compassion* literally means to "suffer with others." In the biblical text for today, Jesus calls his followers to be compassionate people, those who make room in their spirits to offer generous hospitality to others.

A friend of mine, Rita Anton, was the recipient of such kindness, and it has had a warm, lingering effect upon her. After her beloved husband died, Rita volunteered to work with a mission group in Asia.

On one occasion, she was in the airport at Kathmandu, Nepal. She had used up all of her Nepali money to purchase a ticket to Calcutta. Rita was filled with anxiety because she was a woman traveling alone. Many Americans were victims of muggings.

When she reached the airline desk to have her ticket validated, the clerk said, "That will be sixty rupees: airport tax."

"I was sunk," Rita recalls. "They would not accept American money, and it meant I would have to locate a place where some cash could be converted. I had very little time before my flight."

Desperately, she turned to glance at the couple behind her. A very distinguished gentleman in traditional clothing stood with his wife, who wore a beautiful silk sari. "Can you lend me sixty rupees for the tax?" Rita asked boldly. Without hesitation, the gentleman gave her one hundred rupees. She paid the tax, and tried to give him the change. "Oh, no," he said with a warm smile. "You may want to buy a cup of tea in the airport. You keep the change."

Rita asked the man for his address so she could repay him, but the gentleman refused to give it to her saying, "That is not necessary. I am glad to help you."

"I learned he was from Calcutta," Rita says. "His kindness removed the dread I felt. If Calcutta produced people like him, I had nothing to fear. And sure enough, I spent ten days in Calcutta without difficulty."

PRAYER

Loving God, help me expand the boundaries of my heart and soul. Let me reach out and touch others with your love. Amen.

AFFIRMATIONS

Today I will be aware of another person who is struggling.

Today I will respond boldly to the need of another person.

Today I will make room in my heart for the hurt of another person.

REFLECTION

For the Christian there is no such thing as a stranger. There is only the neighbor…the person near us and needing us.
Edith Stein